Participatory Action Research

POCKET GUIDES TO
SOCIAL WORK RESEARCH METHODS

Series Editor
Tony Tripodi, DSW
Professor Emeritus, Ohio State University

HAL A. LAWSON
JAMES C. CARINGI
LORETTA PYLES
JANINE M. JURKOWSKI
CHRISTINE T. BOZLAK

Participatory Action Research

OXFORD
UNIVERSITY PRESS

OXFORD

UNIVERSITY PRESS

Oxford University Press is a department of the University of Oxford.
It furthers the University's objective of excellence in research,
scholarship, and education by publishing worldwide.

Oxford   New York

Auckland   Cape Town   Dar es Salaam   Hong Kong   Karachi
Kuala Lumpur   Madrid   Melbourne   Mexico City   Nairobi
New Delhi   Shanghai   Taipei   Toronto

With offices in

Argentina   Austria   Brazil   Chile   Czech Republic   France   Greece
Guatemala   Hungary   Italy   Japan   Poland   Portugal   Singapore
South Korea   Switzerland   Thailand   Turkey   Ukraine   Vietnam

Oxford is a registered trademark of Oxford University Press
in the UK and certain other countries.

Published in the United States of America by
Oxford University Press
198 Madison Avenue, New York, NY 10016

© Oxford University Press 2015

A copy of this book's Catalog-in-Publication Data is on file
with the Library of Congress
ISBN 978-0-19-020438-9

Contents

Acknowledgments

We appreciate the guidance and support provided by Toni Tripodi, the series editor, and Agnes Bannigan, our consulting editor. We also were guided by three external reviewers who provided insightful criticism and important suggestions.

We also appreciate two graduate students' contributions. The University at Albany's Joe Chiarenzelli provided research assistance related to institutional review boards. The University of Montana's Jean "Ali" Church did the lion's share of the work on organizing the references.

A variety of funding agencies supported our work, and we remain grateful to their respective program officers. For example, the work on design teams (see chapter 2) initially was supported by the Children's Bureau, U.S. Department of Health and Human Services. Communities for Healthy Living (see chapter 4) was supported by the National Institutes of Health (CHL: NIH R24MD0044865). The postdisaster work in Haiti (see chapter 5) was supported by the National Science Foundation (Grant 1133264 of the Disaster Resilience in Rural Communities Program).

Above all, we are grateful to the countless people we have worked with and learned from in our respective participatory action research initiatives. This book would not have been possible without their participation, teaching and guidance, contingent feedback, patience and tolerance, engagement, expertise, and service as co-researchers.

Introduction

Hal A. Lawson

Participatory action research (PAR) is a special investigative methodology. It connects and integrates five priorities. First, PAR enables democratic participation in real-world problem-solving by local stakeholders who typically lack formal research training and credentials when the research begins. Second, this democratic participation occurs in successive action research cycles, which can be described simply as plan, do, study, and act. Third, new knowledge and understanding are generated as local problem-solving proceeds, thus qualifying PAR as research (e.g., Chevalier & Buckles, 2013; Foster-Fishman & Watson, 2011; Stringer, 2014). Fourth, this practice-generated knowledge responds to practitioners' and policymakers' knowledge needs because relevant, useful knowledge for policy and practice is derived from them.

Fifth, PAR's patently local knowledge provides a safeguard against an impending threat associated with globalization—namely, practice and policy homogenization (Lawson, 2011). Homogenization is rooted in part in mainstream researchers' claims about the wholesale generalizability of the knowledge gained from their investigations, and it is facilitated by the worldwide movement toward evidence-based policy and practice. Granting the importance, indeed the strengths, associated with this international development, there are manifest risks and dangers when local voices, choices, and knowledge are neglected, ignored, and discounted. Under these circumstances, rigorous research knowledge has the potential to serve as an instrument for domination, marginalization, and oppression. And when these conditions prevail, research-based knowledge has the potential to cause harm in the name of doing good work. PAR's expressly local knowledge for locally tailored solutions thus provides an important safeguard and a quality assurance mechanism for policy and practice.

This fifth priority is controversial in the research community, and it introduces an inescapable reality. In American social work, and also in related helping disciplines such as education, public health, and community psychology, PAR sparks controversy. PAR challenges conventional research because it entails multiple changes in its conception and implementation.

This book provides relevant details about PAR's challenges and the changes it entails. Compared to conventional research, PAR's changes start with the definition of a researcher. They include new criteria for determining and evaluating knowledge. They extend to alterations in the research-related division of labor (e.g., basic researchers, applied researchers, intervention researchers, practitioners, policymakers, laypersons). What's more, PAR brings fresh perspectives on the relationship between research and practice, especially the extent to which the empirical knowledge derived from conventional research and the theories it constitutes are wholly generalizable to the diverse, complex, and messy worlds of local practice and policy.

Why elect and implement PAR? PAR oftentimes is the method of choice when five conditions prevail: (a) local problems are ripe with uncertainty, complexity, and novelty, and dilemmas must be addressed; (b) there are no easy answers or ready-made solutions; (c) local people called stakeholders have unique expertise about the problem; (d) problem understanding and problem-solving solutions depend on the engagement of these local stakeholders so that their expertise can be tapped; and (e) problem-solving requires an experimental mindset and successive iterations structured by successive PAR phases.

Salient details are provided in the chapters that follow. PAR is defined, explained, justified, and situated in particular contexts. PAR also is contrasted selectively with other research alternatives, especially so in chapter 1. In all such instances, there is a clear and predictable bias toward literature from the United States.

Readers also should know that consensus on a definition of PAR is not easy to achieve. Indeed, nearly every definition of PAR invites some disagreement and controversy. These unavoidable, contested features recommend a suitable introduction for newcomers to PAR. This introductory chapter is structured accordingly. It provides a framework for appreciating and understanding PAR. Like different frames for the same painting, this framework is selective. It illuminates some of PAR's distinctive features, while risking insufficient attention to others. All books focused on PAR have this inherent limitation.

Two kinds of PAR details are provided next. First, PAR is situated in a research context. *Action research,* broadly defined, describes this context. After action research is introduced, the other research alternatives in this framework are presented briefly. Together these research alternatives are like relatives in a family system. Related in fundamental ways, they also are different. They also help to define and describe PAR in another important way. They indicate what PAR is not!

STARTING WITH THE CONTEXT: PARTICIPATORY ACTION RESEARCH'S "RESEARCH RELATIVES"

Five close research relatives are sketched next. They begin with action research, and they include action science, participatory research, community-based participatory research, and intervention research, especially the kind called design and development research.

All five are important. Each has special advantages. Each provides a research alternative that provides special avenues to useful knowledge for policy and practice. Individually and together they facilitate a preliminary understanding of PAR's roots, and they also help to define PAR's boundaries and special parameters. Granting these methods' familial relations with PAR, it also will become apparent that each is unique. Methodological choices are required, and the following analysis introduces and frames them.

The Action Research Foundation

Action research arguably is the mother of this research family system. In other words, action research came first. PAR and the other relatives came later. In fact, some PAR-related controversies are rooted in core disagreements about action research.

Action research can be traced to the pioneering work of Kurt Lewin (1951). Lewin is the same intellectual leader credited with founding the discipline of social psychology. Impatient with basic research that yielded only analytical, understanding-oriented knowledge, Lewin insisted on research that provided knowledge for action.

Lewin's successors later coined a special term for this special knowledge. They called it *actionable knowledge* (e.g., Argyris, 1996; see also St. John, 2013). They also reinforced what would become one of action research's main claims: *Knowledge for practice must be derived from practice.* This pragmatic claim connects action research to the philosophy known as pragmatism and its main proponent, John Dewey.

With action research, "the knowing is in the doing" because practice, suitably framed, offers two important opportunities-as-benefits. First and foremost, it subjects knowledge to an instrumental test. The question is, Does it work as planned to achieve desired outcomes?

At the same time, when action research is embedded in practice and policy, it has the potential to generate new knowledge. Knowledge generation is facilitated under several related conditions: (a) when desired outcomes are achieved; (b) when these outcomes are not achieved, especially when unintended and undesirable outcomes result; (c) when new, challenging circumstances surround and complicate practice and policy; and (d) when the policy and practice problems are embedded in unique local contexts and no tested solutions are readily available.

Lewin's action research was developed with these needs in mind. Striving for a unified approach to knowledge generation and knowledge use, Lewin (1951) offered a revolutionary claim: *The best way to understand and gain knowledge about any phenomenon is by trying to change it in its naturally occurring contexts.* Drawing on this foundation, action research has been progressively formalized and systematized over the last 65 years.

A promising development in one light, in another the action research literature has become more challenging and complicated because a range of alternatives has developed. In brief, the compelling idea of action research for actionable knowledge is subject to multiple meanings and interpretations. Even with some consensus on the need for research that marries knowledge and action, the range of alternatives called action research often is confusing and even bewildering. Persons interested in exploring this claim should start by reviewing *The Handbook of Action Research* (Reason & Bradbury, 2001). Although the variety of action research methods offered in this pioneering volume is impressive and instructive, the manifest diversity nearly always causes confusion.

Another example indicates a revolutionary action research turn. The field of education, especially teacher education, emphasizes routinely a particular view of action research. *Practitioner action research*, especially teacher action research, proceeds with structured methodological guidelines for how individual teachers can research their practice as the practice (e.g., Mills, 2013).

In this view, learning to teach and actually teaching are structured by iterative and recursive action research cycles. The action research cycle, oversimplified in service of clarity, can be summarized as follows: Plan first; then do (act); then study (assess-evaluate); next, reflect on data-as-findings (to gain knowledge); and then do it all again—that is, plan, do, study, reflect. The idea is for teachers to be a special kind of researcher—action researchers who gain knowledge for their practice from their practice—in the successive iterations that constitute their work with students.

In the same vein, pioneering examples of action research, including participatory action research, are offered as clinical practice strategies for work with clients. A relatively recent example provided by Smith & Romero (2010) provides a case in point. In this perspective, another important opportunity is presented—empowerment theory can be joined to PAR-as-direct practice (e.g., Cattaneo & Chapman, 2010).

Such is the diversity "out there." Unfortunately, there is no escape from it, starting with the diverse interpretations of action research. And this is why it is important to understand the action research context and the several methodological alternatives, such as action science.

Action Science

The action research situation becomes more complicated when the idea of *action science* is introduced. It is used in studies of organizations

(Argyris, 2004; Friedman, 2001). In other words, the organization is the unit of analysis. With action science, people, individually as well as in groups and teams, are viewed as persons in organizational environments. Influenced by their organizations, they also can be given actionable knowledge that enables them to plan and implement improvements via organizational learning mechanisms.

Like other kinds of action research, action science derives from Lewin's conceptual foundation. Like other kinds, it is structured to produce actionable knowledge. However, action science has three keynote characteristics. Together they make action science special.

To begin with, action science is structured and guided by generalizable theory. This theory is called the theory of action perspective (Argyris & Schön, 1996). The second characteristic: It requires specialized researchers whose work is grounded in and guided by this theory. Third, it is predicated on the assumption that the people in the organization being studied are research subjects and participants.

This third characteristic is noteworthy. With action science, the researchers are in control. From start to finish, they determine how the action science investigative game is played, and their game is structured in relation to and guided by the theory of action perspective.

There is nothing inherently wrong with this approach. In fact, it has multiple advantages when it fits local needs and promises to achieve designated purposes. The point is to understand action science, starting with these three characteristics, because they differentiate it from PAR.

There are more such differences. With action science, the researcher produces for participants a special kind of actionable knowledge. This new knowledge frames, describes, and explains organizational members' local situation in innovative ways. Thanks to action science, the researcher is able to paint an organizational picture that results in the so-called enlightenment effect. That is, when presented with the findings, the subjects-participants are expected to say things such as, "We didn't know this about ourselves and our organization. Now that you have prepared us to see ourselves in a new light, we are prepared to do something about our problems."

Of course, nearly every kind of research may yield such an enlightenment effect. Action science is special because its guiding theory (the theory of action perspective) also directs participants to the forces, factors, and actors that account for suboptimal social relations and undesirable outcomes. For example, it emphasizes interpersonal defensive routines, implicit blame and maltreatment cycles, cover-up dynamics, adversarial relations, and other group, team, and organizational flaws and systematic errors (Argyris, 2004; Argyris & Schön, 1996). In addition to identifying, describing, and explaining these flaws and errors, action scientists emphasize that these suboptimal relations and organizational dynamics need to be changed in order for desirable results to be achieved. Action scientists are there to help with the change process. They do so by means of the generalizable theory that guides this kind of research.

Actionable knowledge in service of this kind of organizational improvement thus is action science's special benefit. This main feature places it in the action research family system.

Finally, action science requires dedicated resources, especially for external researcher-consultants. It also takes time as its special sequence unfolds. The sequence is research first, interpret the findings, and, thanks to the enlightenment provided by the researcher, use the findings later. Several such cycles may be needed.

Above all, the action scientist is in control from start to finish. Put differently, the researcher rules according to action science's methodological rules. It shall become apparent that these several features differentiate action science from PAR.

Participatory Research

Participatory research has many aliases, such as participatory evaluation (e.g., Preskill & Jones, 2009) and collaborative inquiry (e.g., Trickett & Espino, 2004). The main idea is what matters: People other than formally trained researchers have good ideas to offer about the research question(s), the actual design, the interpretation of the findings, and how the findings can and should be used. This participatory need-as-opportunity is especially apparent when the researcher ventures into unfamiliar conceptual territory and possesses limited knowledge and understanding (e.g., Cornwall & Jewkes, 1995). Under these circumstances, the researcher needs help, particularly from persons with local knowledge.

Such is the frame of reference for the three defining features of participatory research. They are best presented as action-oriented, procedural guidelines for this kind of research. First: Consult local experts, including some persons whom you will recruit and engage as research participants, before you finalize decisions about your research. Second: Return to these local experts when you are striving to interpret your research findings. Third: If you want your research used in a timely manner, again consult local experts on how best to facilitate the use of research knowledge.

Participatory research can be organized in several ways. Fortunately, published resources are available to guide this innovative work. Detailed articles and books are available for participatory research (e.g., Cargo & Mercer, 2008; Trickett & Espino, 2004) and its close relation, participatory evaluation. They cannot and will not be summarized here. However, two kinds of participatory research—*participatory rural appraisal* and *community-based participatory research*—merit mention here because of the growing involvement of social workers and professionals from other disciplines in international development.

Participatory Rural Appraisal

Chambers' pioneering work sets the standard for participatory rural appraisal (PRA; Chambers, 1997). In Chambers' renderings, PRA starts with special occasions such as campfire gatherings. Each participant is given a turn to speak. Turn-taking is facilitated by the passing of a ceremonial stick. The person with the stick voices ideas and choices while the others listen and learn. As the stick is passed from one person to the next, participation in the project design expands. Knowledge for action is gained in the process. Ideally, basic consensus is achieved, and the work that lies ahead has gained three benefits. It is informed by local, expert knowledge. Indigenous people's participation facilitates culturally competent practice. And, local stakeholders' participation facilitates their commitments and collective engagement in making their preferred solution successful. Such is the power of participation in PRA.

Community-Based Participatory Research

Another close action research family relation is noteworthy because it is possibly the most popular and fastest growing investigative alternative. Its name specifies the place where research participation occurs—in the community. It is called community-based participatory research, and it is known in shorthand as CBPR (Cargo & Mercer, 2008; Sandoval et al., 2011; Sunderland, Catalano, Kendall, McAuliffe, & Chenowether, 2010).

Oftentimes, CBPR involves university-community partnerships (e.g., Israel, Schulz, Parker, & Becker, 1998; Masuda, Creighton, Nixon, & Frankish, 201; Sandoval et al., 2011).

Trickett's (2011) framing of CBPR is especially helpful to persons new to this methodology. He emphasizes that, for some researchers, CBPR is essentially an instrumental strategy. In other words, CBPR is just another tool in the researcher's methodological tool kit. In contrast to this narrow, technical view, Trickett emphasizes that CBPR also can be appreciated and adopted as a personal worldview, one that structures and guides research. In this second approach, CBPR is an identity marker, and preferences for this methodology announce a way of being and becoming in the worlds of research-oriented policy and practice.

CBPR is especially suitable for complex problem-solving. Oftentimes, such problem-solving must proceed at multiple levels (practice, organizational design, and policy). At the same time, it simultaneously must target many units of analysis (e.g., children, elders, families, and neighborhoods). For these reasons and others, this new approach is particularly relevant to community development. It also is applicable to a variety of problem-setting and problem-solving initiatives that require immersion in somewhat unique community contexts. CBPR facilitates this kind of research because it both responds to, and exhibits, considerable complexity. This is one reason why teams of researchers are needed.

Significantly, CBPR has two forms. It is important to understand both and look for the differences. It also is important to consider the choices associated with, and the consequences deriving from, them.

Form 1: Like other kinds of participatory research, community research forums enable *consultation* about the several aspects of the research. Participation-as-consultation—tapping community members' views and soliciting their opinions—is the defining feature. The researchers retain power and authority. Put differently, the investigative game remains theirs and theirs alone. As with all manner of participatory research, participation can be operationalized as a kind of tokenism to satisfy research funders and local politicians. In the worst cases, participation is manipulative and stands as a violation of research ethics.

Form 2: Researchers take the radical turn. *They enfranchise, prepare, and empower representative community members as co-researchers.* Here, community-based participatory research and PAR are united, and the resultant synergy can be potent. Two of this book's chapters (chapters 4 and 5) provide compelling examples.

The Politics of Participatory Research

Finally, a special note-as-caution about PAR, CBPR, and all forms of participatory research is in order. *Participation in research is a political process, not just a technique* (Cornwall, 2008, p. 281). This political dimension implicates important questions regarding whose voices and views are heard and whose are not; the extent to which they are heeded; the uses to which participants' views are put; and the reasons and goals for such participation. These same questions are relevant to PAR. With all manner of participatory research and evaluation methodologies, procedures for stakeholder recruitment, selection, and involvement are politically charged.

Cornwall's (2008) analysis is especially relevant to these questions. She provides a compelling typology for determining whose interests and needs are served by participation. She also provides reminders of the dark side of participation. In some instances, participation amounts to tokenism, and in other instances it is expressively manipulative. These threats implicate the importance of researchers' ethics and their moral obligations to do good work while not causing harms.

Intervention Research With a Design and Development Framework

The action research orientation described here, especially Lewin's long-standing priority for gaining actionable knowledge by trying to change phenomena in naturally occurring contexts, will strike a familiar cord for savvy readers. They will recognize that many of these same assumptions and claims accompany intervention research (e.g., Rothman & Thomas, 2009).

Like action research, intervention research is designed to produce actionable knowledge. As with most kinds of action research, intervention researchers are guided by the scientific method. Intervention researchers also strive to articulate theory for practice and policy.

When a design and development framework is added to intervention research (Rothman & Thomas, 2009), its correspondence to PAR is enhanced. Design and development interventions typically begin with a special target and an initial baseline. Intervention design, development, monitoring, and testing continue until the desired outcomes are achieved. In other words, successive intervention iterations are expected and planned. Each provides a new data baseline and facilitates progress monitoring. If the data are promising and there are grounds for optimism regarding successive iterations of essentially the same intervention, replication and extension studies continue. On the other hand, if the data are not encouraging, the intervention is redesigned. Such is the design and development logic for this kind of research. Significantly, as good work proceeds with people manifesting needs, intervention research produces actionable knowledge.

Granting the intervention research's commonalties and similarities vis-à-vis PAR, intervention research design and development are different. The main difference is that intervention researchers make all of the important research-related decisions. For example, they determine the relevant independent and dependent variables. They also decide whether the research should occur in controlled laboratory-like situations or in real-world contexts. In brief, intervention researchers retain complete power and authority over every aspect of the research investigation. This fundamental feature differentiates it from PAR.

PARTICIPATORY ACTION RESEARCH IN THIS BOOK

Because PAR is rooted in part in Lewin's (1951) pathbreaking ideas, it belongs in the action research family system. However, in comparison to other action research methods, PAR is unique and special in several important respects. This book is structured accordingly—to emphasize PAR's uniqueness and special features, alongside researchers' ability to adapt its designs to achieve specific purposes in special contexts at particular times. The primary aim for this book is to illuminate and describe in some detail PAR's uniqueness, albeit in introductory ways. Far from the final, definitive word on this subject, this book lays a solid foundation for PAR newcomers and novices. Viewed in this way, our book is a prequel for more sophisticated, detailed, and nuanced methodological and theoretical analyses.

The more detailed and sophisticated analyses provided by Burns (2010), Chevalier and Buckles (2013), Greenwood & Levin (2007), Kemmis and McTaggart (2000), Schneider (2014), Stringer (2014), and

Wadsworth (2010) are especially important. If this book achieves its primary aim, these several resources will be more inviting, and readers will be able to benefit completely from them. This book stands apart from conventional books and textbooks focused on PAR. Ours is expressly action oriented. Its constituent chapters provide real-world examples of PAR in action. In our view, there is no better way to introduce PAR to graduate students, early career researchers, and veteran researchers on a quest for alternative research methodologies.

Embracing Participatory Action Research Diversity

To reiterate, the intellectual work of defining PAR by providing firm, nonnegotiable boundaries is inherently challenging because PAR is not a monolith. In other words, PAR's conceptual variations and methodological pluralism must be acknowledged directly and explicitly.

This PAR diversity is an asset and an advantage. For example, the several chapters in this book demonstrate that PAR can be tailored to fit particular research and development needs in special local contexts. These chapters also demonstrate that PAR oftentimes proceeds with needs that are jointly identified by the persons who are expected to use the knowledge gained from PAR. In fact, PAR assumes that these persons are experts regarding these needs.

Because these persons have expertise, representative members need to be prepared and positioned as co-researchers. This means that practitioners, policymakers, service users, students, patients, and others take on new roles and responsibilities. In other words, people from all walks of life are positioned, prepared, and supported as co-researchers. They are not merely "research subjects" in ways that conventional research defines and positions them.

Proceeding with these assumptions and others of like kind, we have made some radical decisions as we have planned and developed this book. We have resisted the most popular approach whereby one or a few authors provide an authoritative rendition of PAR. This approach glosses over PAR differences, so much so that some books risk distorting reality. It also provides accounts that are heavy on analysis and light on practical action. In the end, readers are left with too many questions about what PAR means for them and their work, how they can get started, and what resources they can tap to move ahead. Under these circumstances, newcomers to PAR are not likely to see its salience, appreciate its special conditions, requirements, and constraints, and take the next steps to learn how to implement it.

The Importance of Real-World Participatory Action Research Examples

Our book has been planned in accordance with the foregoing considerations. In contrast to conventional textbooks authored by one or two people, typically ones in which PAR studies are referenced for readers to find and appreciate, we offer real-world alternatives. The titles for the several chapters in this book are evidence of these alternatives. We made the decision to identify the specialist authors of each chapter so that readers are able to contact them directly in order to gain more resources.

However tempting it may be to view this book an edited volume, it is not. It is a collaborative product in every respect. In contrast to edited books with chapters authored by different individuals who rarely if ever review each other's contributions, our book has been developed collaboratively by a true team of experienced PAR researchers. The narrative consistency in the following pages can be attributed to genuine teamwork as we strived to craft the most concise and illuminating introduction to PAR.

In the same vein, our book's multiple authors give concrete expression to the idea of "participatory." Sharing authorship is especially important because it has enabled us to model an important norm for PAR: Co-researchers such as students and community members need to be considered for co-authorship!

Our approach derives from the view that no one person has a monopoly on PAR expertise and how best to conceptualize and implement it. In the same vein, no single academic discipline reigns supreme when PAR is defined and operationalized. In fact, interdisciplinary PAR, including community-based PAR, is on the rise, and we endorse this development.

A superficial examination of the chapter titles indicates such PAR variety, together with appreciation for important differences. Different in so many respects, readers will conclude that these PAR accounts belong together because the core, defining features of PAR—described in chapter 1—are manifest in all of them. Viewed in this way, chapters 2–5 provide important examples of PAR's flexibility and adaptability—that is, ways that researchers can developed tailor-made designs that enable them to achieve their primary purposes.

Toward Expanded Research Methodological Repertoires

We authors are not PAR zealots and advocates who are intent on converting readers to our way of thinking and doing research. All of us have experience with conventional research methodologies. All of us expect to have more such experience in the future.

Our second aim for this book, after illuminating and describing PAR's uniqueness, follows from these admissions. Our second aim is to enable social workers and researchers from other helping disciplines to expand their research repertoires. Note this emphasis on methodological variety and expansion. Our aim is not to pit PAR against all manner of conventional research frameworks and methodologies.

Some PAR advocates do this. They frame the choice of a research methodology as a zero-sum game. Predictably, they conclude that PAR is the clear winner. Not so in this book. PAR is offered as a special methodology that is fit for special purposes, in unique contexts, and at particular times. Valuable as a stand-alone, PAR also can be combined with other research methodologies as part of multiple methods designs or mixed methods designs. Chapters 2 and 4 provide cases in point.

THE RATIONALE FOR THE SUCCEEDING CHAPTERS

Chapter 1 reinforces and builds on this introduction. It provides PAR's defining features, contrasting them with the core features of conventional research. Using a game metaphor, PAR's defining rules and strategies are identified and described briefly. The special needs and problems that invite PAR and may necessitate it are identified, described, and explained.

Once selected comparisons and contrasts are provided, PAR's boundaries become clearer. For example, it will become apparent what PAR is and does; and also the conditions under which it can be a preferred methodology. At the same time, it will become apparent what PAR is not.

Striving for an intellectual balance while preventing overzealous advocacy, chapter 1 provides a research problem typology. The main idea here is that PAR is especially suited for some kinds of research problems—namely, complex adaptive problems and dilemma-rich, wicked ones—but less so for technical problems with available solutions. This claim is especially important, and it sets the stage for the following, companion claim.

No more and no less than every other research methodology, PAR is selective in every respect. Its selectivity is manifest in the kinds of problems it addresses, how it is designed and implemented, and its overall approach to knowledge development and use.

This PAR explication in chapter 1 sets the stage for the other chapters. Each succeeding chapter adds one or more dimensions to the PAR design. Chapters 2 and 3 demonstrate PAR's fit for purpose with adaptive problems. Chapters 4 and 5 illustrate PAR's import for wicked, dilemma-rich, and context-embedded problems. The complexity grows with each chapter.

In chapter 2 Lawson and Caringi focus on PAR in organizations. The focus here is workforce retention in child welfare organizations challenged by pervasive, undesirable, and potentially preventable turnover. The authors describe the formation and operation of special PAR teams called design teams. Examples of the teams' work are provided, and conventional research and evaluation studies of this special PAR design team are cited. Implications for other kinds of organizations are outlined in conclusion.

Bozlak and Kelly provide a compelling example of PAR in chapter 3. Here the practice sector is the intersection of health and education, and these two researchers describe their PAR with school-aged children. As with the design team example in the previous chapter, it is easy to imagine comparable PAR studies with children and youth in a variety of community, organizational, and policy contexts. The special challenges associated with PAR with young people are noteworthy (see also Foster-Fishman, Law, Lichty, & Aoun, 2010; Ozer & Wright, 2012).

In chapter 4, Jurkowski and her colleagues provide an important example of PAR complexity. They join PAR with a community-based participatory research (CBPR) design. Here, the research and development priority is obesity prevention and intervention among vulnerable preschool children and their families—a wicked problem. The authors describe the formation of a community advisory board (CAB) with a special innovation. Targeted parents also are CAB members, and they enjoy equal power and authority with the professionals.

What's more, these CAB parents and selected others are prepared and positioned as co-researchers who employ two innovative research strategies that enable people without formal training to generate and offer new knowledge. These strategies are windshield surveys (parents narrate auto trips through places of interest) and photovoice methods (e.g., Jurkowski, 2008). These PAR methods were used in combination with conventional research methodologies, both quantitative and quantitative. Ultimately, PAR provided action-oriented knowledge not possible via conventional research methods. However, this study included quantitative and qualitative methods. This study's unique combination of many such methods helps to explain its inclusion in this book.

Pyles and Svistova's chapter 5 addresses a particularly important and unusually complex, challenging PAR opportunity. The focus is postdisaster research and development, and the problem cluster earns the descriptor "wicked." The case described involves Haiti, one of the poorest and most marginalized nations in the world before the earthquake and the astounding damage it caused. The PAR initiated by these social work colleagues is inspiring and instructive.

Granting the strengths and the impressive resilience of Haitians after the disaster, they faced challenges aplenty before it. The account provided by Pyles and Svistova thus is not a Cinderella story with miraculous outcomes. Rather, it is an example of how PAR can be an important international development tool, one that enables good people in especially challenging contexts to make demonstrable progress over time. These researchers' small wins, gained through PAR, ultimately may pave the way for huge gains. Granting this ideal possibility, the jury is still out on the huge gains. So, this PAR example is instructive for others interested in research and development initiatives in postdisaster situations and national contexts.

The final chapter provides an action-oriented summary. Here, we authors join forces to provide practical insights into PAR. We emphasize the lessons we have learned as we have ventured into this relatively new

PAR arena. We used an important framing question to derive these PAR lessons. If we researchers knew then—when we launched our PAR—what we know now (after the research), what would we do differently and better? These lessons learned are offered to enable researchers, present and future, to get started on new, much-needed lines of investigation.

This summary chapter also presents PAR-related tensions, conflicts, and controversies. Some are endemic, which means that there is no easy or surefire way to prevent them. For example, conventional researchers raise questions about the validity of knowledge gained from PAR. Another example: What appears to be a direct and relatively easy pathway to knowledge via PAR often materializes as something entirely different once the research has commenced. Endemic tensions and conflicts inevitably emerge. This last chapter provides examples.

Finally, this last chapter introduces strategies for minimizing PAR challenges. For example, the PAR researcher can delimit the investigation. A puzzle metaphor helps to explain delimitations. PAR problem delimitation entails the researcher's decision to focus on just one or two pieces instead of the whole puzzle. As with conventional research, the PAR researchers determine these delimitations. In other words, the researchers impose them.

At the same time, the researchers can explicitly acknowledge the PAR investigation's limitations. In contrast to investigator-imposed delimitations, limitations are endemic in PAR. If fact, some limitations are unavoidable because of the kinds of problems PAR is designed to address and also because persons without extensive, formal training and requisite credentials are co-researchers.

THE FIT WITH SOCIAL WORK PRACTICE

The special import of selected social work practice skills, abilities, and sensitivities in PAR is a unique feature of the analysis that follows. PAR, as described and explained in this book, qualifies as a special kind of social work practice. In fact, the catchy phrase *the social work of participatory action research* is accurate because PAR is a powerful mechanism for gaining knowledge for the social construction and constitution of reality—in serve of humankind.

Other relevant details are provided in chapter 1. For example, PAR's required competencies map nicely on the clinical practice skills required for group work. In the same vein, when PAR is joined with CBPR, research skills and abilities and community-organizing skills and abilities converge.

AN INTERNATIONAL REACH

To reiterate, many of the references and the majority of examples are from the United States. Even so, this book is structured as a resource for social workers and other helping professionals who are located in other nations. A review of the international action research literature indicates that parts of this book are relevant to other parts of the world. To the extent that this claim is valid, social workers and their partners everywhere may enhance their understanding, expand their research competence, and discover new frameworks for, and opportunities associated with, PAR.

Although it is challenging to write for both local and international audiences, it is important to make the effort. After all, social work is "going global" in response to the many human needs, social problems, and policy opportunities that transcend national boundaries (e.g., Lawson, 2011). For example, in the midst of the largest human migration in history, a growing number of social workers, everywhere, are involved in international social work as diverse people from different nations and cultural contexts "mix and match" in new places.

Another example: Disasters now are international events requiring international action, and social workers have pivotal roles to play. Chapter 5, by Pyles and Svistova, is structured accordingly and provides salient details. Pyles and Svistova's work is just the beginning for international social work involving PAR. Needs and opportunities for PAR are manifest in multiple sectors of international work, including the special attention needed for unique national, regional, and local contexts.

Finally, researchers in other helping disciplines will benefit from this book because the kinds of problems described in the several chapters are inherently interdisciplinary and necessitate PAR with interdisciplinary teams. Granting disciplinary competition, what matters most is shared commitments to social and economic justice, human well-being and social welfare, and integrated, sustainable social and economic development. Such is the grand frame of reference for this little book, and it helps to announce the authors' big aspirations for it.

Introducing Participatory Action Research

Hal A. Lawson

INTRODUCTION

The primary aim for this chapter is to describe and explain the defining features of participatory action research (PAR). This chapter thus sets the stage for the real-world PAR examples provided in chapters 2–5. Each succeeding chapter provides additional details regarding methodological alternatives as well as a rationale regarding why and how PAR is a good fit for the presenting problems-as-opportunities.

The secondary aim is to establish an important correspondence between social work and PAR. Although this social work orientation does not rule out other helping fields, it provides a special PAR recommendation for social work because of this profession's historic and enduring commitment to address the antecedents, causes, correlates, and consequences of unjust and harmful poverty, marginalization, social exclusion, domination, and oppression.

This last claim signals an important reminder, and it needs to be made explicit at the outset. Research has the potential to marginalize and exclude vulnerable people, especially those who reside in challenging places. Moreover, research-based knowledge has the potential to silence the voices and choices of vulnerable people. When this occurs, the result is a bitter irony. Research designed to advance the common good ends up being exclusionary, discriminatory, and oppressive, perhaps becoming yet another form of domination.

The potential import of PAR begins with this set of risks, threats, and dangers. When PAR convenes, organizes, and mobilizes vulnerable people in vulnerable places, it provides one safeguard against such a huge ethical violation—that is, when research designed to serve actually causes harm. PAR enables morally guided researchers to honor their social responsibilities.

With these grand ideals in mind, it is important to acknowledge at the outset that PAR is not a research panacea. For example, critics often raise important questions about the validity of knowledge gained from PAR studies (e.g., Waterman, 1998), and others emphasize PAR's inherent tensions and ambiguities (Regher, 2000). All such criticisms are associated with an important, defining feature of PAR—namely, methodological pluralism. In fact, chapters 2–5 are structured to illustrate PAR differences and prepare readers to consider PAR-related alternatives, together with important choices researchers must make. Mindful of this pluralism, the PAR description and explanation provided in this chapter can be characterized as a dominant version. There are other versions.

The ensuing rendition of PAR is selective in another way. Although it is relevant to all helping fields, this analysis is specifically oriented toward social work because PAR corresponds with three of its practice priorities. To begin with, the requirements for lead PAR researchers fit nicely with social workers' group work competencies. In the same vein, when PAR is viewed as a special kind of intervention, there is a good fit with social workers' intervention competencies. Third, because PAR increasingly is part of a comprehensive strategy for community-based, participatory research, it also fits with social work's community practice competencies.

With these points of correspondence in full view, a catchy phrase has salience. The phrase is "the social work of participatory action research." This descriptor is accurate because PAR is a special kind of social work practice characterized by simultaneous knowledge generation and progressive problem-solving as groups of researchers engage in the social construction of reality. *PAR is indeed social work!*

Chapter 1 proceeds as follows: The first section draws on a social work practice principle; that is, start where the client is—in this case, where the reader is. A real-world thought experiment provides this invitational opportunity. Next, because every solid, useful definition of a construct starts with what the construct is, the second section of this chapter provides a thick description of PAR. It is described as a systematic investigative game with formal rules. Finally, a companion priority is to identify and describe what PAR is not. The third section is structured accordingly. It provides selective comparisons and contrasts between PAR and conventional research, setting the stage for a conclusion, one that provides some important questions and an organizational framework for research.

A THOUGHT EXPERIMENT: EXPLORING RESEARCH MEANINGS AND ALTERNATIVES

A thought experiment adapted from Abbott's (2001) analysis of the academic disciplines provides a good start to exploring research alternatives. This little experiment is used every year in the first meeting of a graduate seminar focused on action research and action theories. Give it a try.

You have been selected to join a team of researchers. A team is needed because your charge is very ambitious. Your team's research mission is to describe and explain all relevant aspects of a large city such as neighborhood cultures and composition, how people interact with each other, where businesses are located, and how social needs and problems may cluster in particular places. In other words, your team is charged with painting a complete and accurate picture based on research. There are no immediate restrictions. Your team can be as large as you need it to be, and you have an enormous amount of money for your research.

The question is, How will you design your research in order to produce the best findings?

A Patterned Response Based on a Dominant Idea of Research

Students in these seminars immediately do some impressive, collective brainstorming, and their work stands as testimony to dramatic improvements in master's-level and doctoral research methods classes. Typically, they start by suggesting large-scale surveys with representative samples. Then, they recommend using available data sources because of the bountiful opportunities they offer for secondary data analysis.

Before too long, students interested in qualitative research chime in. They emphasize the need to interview the city's residents in order to gain knowledge about people's socially constructed meanings and experiences. Next, some students emphasize the need to hear the voices and views of marginalized and oppressed city residents. Their priority typically leads to others' preference for a place-based research strategy, involving purposive sampling of the places where social and economic disadvantage and hardship are concentrated and relying on the postal service's zip codes for sampling purposes.

These several examples remind students with anthropology backgrounds about the importance of ethnographic studies that emphasize the cultural aspects of city life. Other students then suggest studies of voter behavior, especially voter turnout, because city politics matter. Ultimately, students begin to wonder about changes over time, and so they add a historical component to the research design. Readers, no doubt, can offer other alternatives.

In this impressive, progressive fashion, students collectively design a large-scale research study with multiple methods. When pressed for the rationale for their preferred method's inclusion, students accurately emphasize the selectivity of the other methods. They argue persuasively that every research method is selective. They also argue that a research-based depiction of the city will not be sufficiently comprehensive, complete, and accurate unless *their* preferred method is included and the findings derived from it are emphasized.

All in all, students demonstrate considerable expertise in *research as social analysis*. In other words, they show that they have learned and internalized the dominant view of science as impartial, objective observation. Moreover, they are vigilant in their efforts to guard against personal bias and threats of research contamination.

Recurrent, Predictable Selectivity Regarding Research

Students' selectivity in the way they conceptualize research is manifest in how they talk about research, how they envision its implementation, and what they count as valid, reliable, and useful knowledge. Significantly, Kurt Lewin's (1951) bold claim rarely materializes in this thought experiment. Recall that this claim was presented in the introduction to the book, and it bears repeating here: "The best way to understand and gain knowledge about any phenomenon is by trying to change it in its naturally occurring contexts." In short, why not try to change aspects of the city in order to gain knowledge and understanding about it? Initially, students do not consider this possibility.

In the same vein, it does not occur to students that research can proceed with the dual purpose of gaining new knowledge and at the same time that people from several walks of life strive to address a significant local problem. Moreover, it does not occur to students that laypeople without research credentials—practitioners, laypersons, and policymakers—can be prepared and positioned as co-researchers charged with improving some aspect of city life.

In the main, students have been prepared to think about research as a valuable resource, indeed an essential one for practitioners and policymakers. Their professors have continued to drum a big idea into their heads: Best practices and policies are based on research. The controversial idea that conventional research and the knowledge it yields has the potential to become dominant and even oppressive, ruling out people's local knowledge and silencing their voices, is not immediately on students' perceptual radar screens.

Another void is apparent. Although students are prepared to use empowerment theory in their practice, it never occurs to them that this same theory can inform research and guide researchers. In their initial view, research-as-social analysis is one thing. Empowerment practice is another. In this dominant view, empowerment is what happens when practitioners, policymakers, and laypersons use the research knowledge generated for them by specially prepared, credentialed, anointed, and sponsored researchers.

Consequently, it is wholly predictable that students are not prepared to connect laypersons', practitioners', and policymakers' direct engagement in research—as co-researchers who cogenerate knowledge and at the same time address and begin to solve important problems—to empowerment theory and practice. In the same vein, the idea of *researcher as scholar change agent* is a revolutionary idea because conventional research methods courses emphasize the social distancing of researchers from social actors, their social actions, and their social situations.

DESCRIBING, EXPLAINING, AND JUSTIFYING PARTICIPATORY ACTION RESEARCH

PAR provides the opportunity to explore, implement, and elaborate a revolutionary idea. It has the potential to recast researchers' roles, empowering researchers as scholar change agents. They are both scholars and change agents because PAR joins social analysis and social action, bringing both to bear on knowledge production in service of practical problem-solving.

Insofar as knowledge is power, and laypeople both generate and use PAR knowledge, scholar change agents who facilitate PAR are able to frame, name, and conduct their work as a special kind of empowerment practice. Because groups are involved, and group members empower one another, PAR can become a relational empowerment practice (Christens, 2012).

Methodological Pluralism: The Three Keywords

PAR joins three important ideas: research, action, and participation. Each is important in its own right. Each also is subject to multiple meanings, definitions, and interpretations. This plurality of meaning, definition, and interpretation is especially evident with *participation* and *research.*

When these three ideas are joined in PAR, there is a predictable consequence. More meanings, definitions, interpretations, and proposed uses are generated by the tripartite PAR descriptor. This is one reason why methodological pluralism is evident in the diverse ways that PAR is practiced and written about in diverse parts of the world. This conceptual and operational pluralism is compounded by endemic conflicts regarding the standards and rules for acceptable, rigorous PAR practice. For example, serious disagreement surrounds an important methodological issue—that is, is PAR structured in relation to and guided by the scientific method (Greenwood & Levin, 2007)? Answers vary. In the past, the answer depended on the researchers' location. At one time, researchers in the Northern Hemisphere proceeded with the scientific method, and their research tended to focus on organizations and their improvement. Meanwhile, their colleagues in the Southern Hemisphere were engaged in grassroots PAR for social movements. Women's rights movements and workers' rights and literacy movements stand as two prominent examples. For these community-based PAR initiatives, the scientific method was not necessary. In fact, it was viewed as a luxury. This basic distinction based on researchers' location in the world lingers in the literature. Even so, both kinds of PAR (i.e., with and without the scientific method) can be found everywhere.

There are still other differences in PAR practice. Unfortunately, there is no escape from this potentially confusing and somewhat dismaying state of affairs. As the PAR literature grows, and PAR practice expands worldwide, there will be more variability, methodological innovation, and controversy. The following bold claim provides a firm point of departure: PAR is not a monolith. The implication, perhaps obvious, needs to be emphasized. PAR researchers need to make informed choices. The selective snapshot that follows is offered in service of this need, and the chapters that follow support and extend the need for informed choices.

A Dominant Perspective on the Participatory Action Research Investigative Game

In one of the dominant versions of PAR, co-researchers are guided by the scientific method (e.g., Foster-Fishman & Watson, 2011; Greenwood & Levin, 2007). Consensus on this important criterion is not apparent, however, and there is little reason to believe that it will develop in the near future.

There is growing consensus on another criterion. Like other formal research methods, PAR is structured in relation to, and later evaluated by, formal rules. This is one reason why some analysts liken research, especially scientific research, to a formal game (e.g., McCain & Segal, 1982). The researchers (players) seek to advance knowledge by following methodological rules and adhering to ethical standards.

It follows that the rules of the investigative game need to be understood in order for informed choices to be made and also for the game to be played properly. Two related rule structures are especially important (Searle, 1995). The *constitutive rules* of a research method provide its boundaries. In other words, a research method's constitutive rules serve to define it and to differentiate it from other methods. These rules are like boundaries that indicate what the method is and also what it is not. For example, the constitutive rules for a causal-comparative design differentiate it from the constitutive rules for a quasi-experimental design. In turn, the constitutive rules for a quasi-experimental design differentiate it from an ethnographic design.

In contrast, a research method's *regulative rules* provide attitudinal norms, behavioral scripts, and research implementation strategies. These rules stipulate how each investigative game must be played in order for the findings to merit the status of valid, reliable, and useful knowledge. So it is with PAR. It has formal constitutive rules as well as regulative rules.

Continuing with the same metaphor, investigative game playing is evaluated by referees. The relevant reminder here is that research and scholarship in every discipline are collective endeavors, that is, they are peer governed and peer evaluated (Kuhn, 1996). Peer evaluations can be implemented because multiple players work in the same specialties in order to advance the frontiers of knowledge. Knowledge advances as scholarly and scientific peers evaluate an investigator's research method and "certify" its knowledge claims.

Significantly, every method's regulative and constitutive rules are instrumental in these peer evaluations. That is, all peer evaluations are structured by basic important questions about the extent to which the researchers have followed the rules of their respective investigative games. If they did not play the game properly—that is, they did not implement the constitutive and regulative rules competently—academic peers serving as referees will question and debunk the researchers' knowledge claims. Toward this end, graduate study in every discipline is directed in part at students' abilities to make informed evaluations about the quality and fidelity of scientific and scholarly game playing. PAR fits squarely in this context. Its constitutive and regulative rules provide operational guidelines for researchers as well as evaluative criteria for the evaluation of PAR studies.

Participatory Action Rules

When PAR is framed and named as a research game, it can be defined, explained, and evaluated by means of its constitutive and regulative rules. These two sets of rules are presented in Figure 1.1. To reiterate, PAR constitutive rules serve to identify PAR boundaries, and its regulative rules stipulate its research strategies. Together, these two sets of rules introduce what PAR is and, by implication, what it is not.

These rules indicate what researchers must know and be able to do when they opt for PAR and implement it. In other words, they introduce what it takes to become a competent PAR investigative game player. These rules also serve two other functions. They enable newcomers to PAR to undertake criterion-referenced (rule-structured) reviews and evaluations of published PAR studies. At the same time, rule commonalities are manifest in these studies, and so are some important differences. As with all differences in research rules, these manifest differences are consequential. For example, it matters if PAR is structured in relation to, and guided by, the scientific method. It is important to look for such differences and come to terms with the knowledge-related consequences stemming from each study's uniqueness.

Fine-grained discriminations like these enable researchers to make several informed decisions. For example, is the knowledge provided by a PAR study valid, reliable, and useful? Should my multiple methods research design include PAR? If so, what kind of PAR? If not, what method might be a better choice, and what criteria need to be considered in making this decision? Although these questions privilege PAR, they are relevant to every study.

An Experimental Mindset With Considerable Persistence and Resilience

With PAR, knowledge-generating research and practical problem-solving activities in local contexts occur simultaneously. PAR typically

Constitutive Rules: The Defining Features of PAR

➤ The research problem (phenomenon of interest) that necessitates and launches PAR is not wholly understood, and ready-made solutions apparently are not available.

➤ Especially when PAR is structured in relation to, and guided by, the scientific method, rigorous reviews of related research are expected and prerequisite to the study's launch.

➤ PAR is an optimal research strategy for developing clarity about, and knowledge for, this phenomenon of interest because the best way to understand the problem is by trying to change it in its naturally occurring context(s).

➤ PAR is conducted in real world, natural settings.

➤ Persons without substantial research training, experience, demonstrated competence and formal credentials have valuable expertise regarding the phenomenon of interest, and enlightening knowledge generation depends on their engagement in PAR-structured problem-solving. Consequently, laypersons (including clients, patients, students and service users), practitioners, and policy makers are designated as co-researchers.

➤ Laypersons, practitioners, and policy makers serving as co-researchers must be prepared for PAR, and the lead researcher(s) possessing formal training and credentials must provide this preparation, accompanying social supports, and requisite resources.

➤ PAR, like group work, team development, and networked communities of practice, fundamentally depends on the lead researchers' abilities to organize and mobilize co-researchers for collective action, especially the ability to facilitate the investigative process over time, managing conflicts, and developing "win-win" strategies that unite participants.

➤ PAR, like group work, team development, and networked communities of practice, fundamentally depends on special social settings with supportive prescriptive and prohibitive norms that enhance participant interactions, while safeguarding the quality of treatment each participant experiences.

➤ Democratic decision-making about all relevant aspects of the research is the norm, and lead researchers are responsible for initially established shared decision-making structures and processes.

➤ PAR is an iterative and recursive research process structured by a clear purpose (oftentimes operationalized as SMART goals) and structured cycles of inquiry that enable collective, action learning, incremental knowledge development, problem-solving progress, and adjustments in hypothesized problem-solving solutions.

➤ Research-based solutions to the problem are not expected to be generalizable. That is, what works for one person-, group-team, family-, organization-, community-, and town-city may not work for others.

Figure 1.1 PAR's Constitutive and Regulative Rules.

> However, the PAR process may be generalizable, and so considerable attention to, and careful documentation of, the research phases and details is essential.

> If the research is presented at scholarly-academic meetings and published in journals and books, representative co-researchers who have made special contributions are expected to be co-authors.

> In contrast to the passive voice used to describe most conventional research, researchers use an active voice to describe who did what; when, where, how, and why; and the research outcomes, both intended and unintended.

> Evaluate the findings with regarding to a special kind of theory: A theory of change, also known as a theory of action.

Regulative Rules: PAR Strategies

> Draw on a review of the related research as you frame and plan the PAR investigation and the accompanying co-researcher recruitment and capacity-building processes.

> If you intend to publish the research, complete the application process for the Institutional Review Board.

> Gain as much advanced knowledge as possible about the relationship between the research problem and the people with expertise about it, especially the people who must act strategically and effectively to address the problem.

> Do your homework on the targeted people and their affiliations: Start with the best determinations of the right mix of the essential people.

> Develop PAR training and learning materials, ensuring that participants are adequately prepared for the investigative journey before it commences.

> Start small, on a manageable scale, with consensus on the research purpose and where the probability of demonstrable, immediate progress is high.

> Ensure that all participants agree on the main research question(s), especially the language that will be used to define, describe and address it.

> From start to finish, emphasize the need for and importance of actionable knowledge, insisting that proposed solutions are ones that can be tried out immediately and evaluated in practice.

> Ensure that all participants enjoy voice and choice regarding every aspects of the research investigation, which means that the lead researcher(s) must share power and control whenever possible.

> Because every perspective and alternative strategy ultimately may have merit and use-values, develop an idea parking lot, which provides a storage space for priorities, alternatives, and strategies that are not top priorities or may not be feasible at this time.

Figure 1.1 (Continued)

➤ Establish firmly group norms and operational procedures. For example, agree that PAR language must be strengths-based and solution-focused with companion rules for preventing deficit-oriented thinking as well as finger-pointing and blaming dynamics. (See attached Figure 3.)

➤ Make sure that everyone understands that conflict is unavoidable and, if handled properly, generates good ideas. Develop consensus on the use of dialogue instead of divisive debates (see attached description in Figure 4).

➤ All decisions must be "data driven," which recommends a formal process such as the development of logic models to guide PAR iterations and decision-making.

➤ Keep meticulous records of all meetings because they are essential "data" to be used in monitoring progress and building the group's collective efficacy.

➤ Honor prior achievements and reward "small wins" to keep participants engaged and maintain the PAR momentum.

➤ Develop procedures that ensure that, even while every voice is heard and also that problem-solving dialogue is focused, detailed, efficient, and productive.

➤ Whenever and wherever possible, start with SMART goals (i.e., goals that are strategic and specific; measurable, attainable, results-based, and time-bound).

➤ Because short-term obstacles and permanent barriers to success are predictable, develop appropriate strategies and contingency plans in anticipation of these challenges because they have the potential to derail the PAR effort

➤ Do not try to solve complex adaptive and wicked problems in one effort: Where possible and feasible, chunk out solvable aspects of these problems.

➤ Identify and develop continuous monitoring and continuous quality improvement mechanisms such identifying and celebrating small wins, addressing obstacles and barriers; and adapting the PAR to meet new needs.

➤ Change the PAR participants as circumstances change, perhaps adding new members or reducing the number of participants.

➤ Especially when complex problems must be addressed, structure sub-groups and special task forces for particular aspects of these problems.

➤ Especially when research publication is a priority, subject the study and its findings to collective, democratic evaluations and "proofs"—and make sure that the authorship is based on group consensus.

Figure 1.1 (Continued)

takes time. Because it addresses special kinds of problems, which are ripe with uncertainty, novelty, and complexity, PAR requires an experimental mind-set. Moreover, PAR requires considerable persistence and resilience because there are no easy, ready answers for the kinds of problems it addresses. Knowledge generation occurs over time, and it is structured by formal research cycles.

Participatory Action Research Cycles

In contrast to "one and done" conventional research studies, PAR proceeds via successive, formally structured action research cycles. For example, it takes several PAR iterations for researchers to come to terms with the problem they are trying to solve. The simplest way to describe the PAR research cycle is by means of four action-oriented words: plan, do, study, act. However, the simplest depictions often are misleading. (To avoid misunderstanding, readers are encouraged to review the multiple depictions of the PAR cycle available at the following link: https://www.google.com/search?q=action+research+cycles&tbm=isch&tbo=u&source=univ&sa=X&ei=UESCUqL3O6byyAGi1IGwBQ&sqi=2&ved=0CC4QsAQ&biw=1920&bih=985.)

There are two defining features of PAR: (a) It is an iterative process. Each cycle builds on the previous one(s). (b) It is also a recursive process. Each cycle's knowledge contributions provide timely opportunities to reflect on where participants started, taking stock of all that they have learned and the knowledge and understanding they have produced along the way.

Phases, not Steps

Although some PAR experts present these cycles as a series of steps, there are limitations to this approach. Steps amount to scripted sequences based on linear causal logic and with the expectation that rigid compliance is required. This is industrial age thinking. In view of the attendant limitations of this industrial age thinking and planning, *phases* is a better term to describe these inquiry cycles. Phases are nonlinear, and they are recommended with due recognition that there is an endemic, desirable "back and forth" when PAR is designed to address vexing problems.

Two Views of Participatory Action Research Cycles

With this extensive variation in mind, two cycles dominate the literature and PAR practice. The first cycle begins with the problem identification phase, followed by planning (developing a proposed solution), then implementing the solution, and then monitoring and evaluating outcomes, which paves the way for *reflection on action* (described in the next section).

The second structured cycle builds on the first, but augments it with three additional phases: (a) a literature review, (b) data collection, and (c) data interpretation. This emphasis on data is especially important in forms of PAR conducted in accordance with the scientific method—and with the reminder that not all PAR is guided by the scientific method.

Reflection in Action and Reflection on Action

Oftentimes PAR investigators rely on formal methods for *reflection in action* (Schön, 1983) and post hoc *reflection on action* (Seibert & Daudelin, 1999). Both kinds of knowledge-focused reflection enable simultaneous learning, knowledge generation, and problem-solving. Put another way, PAR investigators must skillfully and simultaneously juggle three main priorities. They pursue formal knowledge as they strive to meet needs and solve problems and monitor whether they are achieving desired outcomes.

Four Knowledge Priorities

Thanks to such structured, purposeful, iterative, and recursive interactions among the co-researchers, each PAR cycle generates new knowledge. Employing intervention language, these knowledge gains are pertinent to four priorities:

- Determinations of the defining features of the problem(s) being addressed (i.e., the theory of the problem);
- Determinations of efficient and effective problem-solving models and strategies (i.e., the intervention that best fits the problem);
- Determinations of potential, replicable operational pathways to desirable outcomes (oftentimes called theories of action or theories of change);
- Determinations of special conditions and unique circumstances in local contexts, which together account for PAR outcomes, perhaps constraining and preventing generalizability of the findings.

This fourth potential contribution needs more elaboration. Although the knowledge gained from a PAR investigation may not stand the test of time and may not be generalizable from one place to another, the

PAR *process* and *research design* may be generalizable. Put differently, to the extent that identical and similar problems need to be addressed in unique local contexts, a formally structured PAR investigative process may merit replication, extension, and scale-up.

Authentic, Democratic Participation

PAR depends on local stakeholders' genuine participation in knowledge generation intertwined with real-world problem-solving. This local stakeholder participation is needed for three reasons. Practitioners, laypersons, and policymakers have essential expertise to offer about the nature of the problem. They also have expertise about potential solutions. What's more, project success depends on their active engagement in implementing and evaluating solutions that yield desirable outcomes.

Viewed in this way, PAR unites democratic citizenship with research-structured knowledge generation. This is why politically savvy researchers link PAR to the requirements and demands of democratic citizenship. More succinctly, PAR is a political act, because it organizes and mobilizes citizens for research-driven collective action. Because PAR emphasizes this citizen mobilization and participation in ways conventional research typically does not, the fit between political democracy and research is one of PAR's unique features (Chevalier & Buckles 2013; Greenwood & Levin, 2007; Kemmis & McTaggart, 2000).

PAR-related empowerment strategies and outcomes, facilitated by scholar change agents, follow suit. The knowledge generated by PAR paves the way for empowering political participation and action in service of social change. Such are the unique features of PAR.

Recasting Researchers' Roles, Responsibilities, and Relationships with Participants

With PAR, co-researchers from various walks of life actively coproduce desirable outcomes, and, as they do, they cogenerate knowledge (Greenwood & Levin, 2007). For this to happen systematically in service of valid, reliable, and useful knowledge, these co-researchers must be prepared. Formally prepared and credentialed researchers are able to provide this preparation for laypersons, practitioners, and policymakers, and they also offer social supports, technical assistance, and relevant research resources throughout.

In response to these manifest needs, PAR recasts researchers' roles, responsibilities, and especially their relationships with laypeople. To begin with, PAR has firm requirements associated with research participants. In brief, PAR does not permit a bypass for the requirements for participants in research. For example, evaluations by institutional review boards are expected, and guidance increasingly is available in the budding literature (e.g., Brown et al., 2010; Shore, Drew, Brazauskas, & Seifer, 2011).

Above all, lead PAR researchers must prepare laypeople people without extensive research training and credentials for structured research. This inclusive strategy flies in the face of the dominant form of research, in which the investigator exclusively conducts the investigation. In contrast, PAR has the potential to empower co-researchers.

For a credentialed, specialist researcher, this work involves three roles: (a) lead researcher; (b) empowering teacher and capacity builder; and, owing to the first two, (c) scholar change agent, who facilitates intertwined knowledge generation and progressive problem-solving in service of the human condition.

Alongside these roles are several important responsibilities. For example, PAR investigators in lead roles must select special methods that diverse people from different walks of life can learn quickly and employ skillfully. They also must rely on communication mechanisms (especially language systems) accessible to people without doctoral degrees or advanced training in formal research methods. Moreover, these researchers have primary responsibility for helping PAR groups develop prosocial norms, feasible and efficient operational procedures, and conflict resolution mechanisms. For example, debate induces conflict, whereas dialogue promotes group cohesion (Roulier, 2000), as illustrated in Figure 1.2.

In the same vein, securing and maintaining a social setting conducive to successive iterations of PAR with robust participation by all participants is another special responsibility (Seidman, 2012), as discussed in chapters 2–5.

Dialogue is collaborative: two or more sides work together toward common understanding.
Debate is oppositional: two sides oppose each other and attempt to prove each other wrong.

In dialogue, finding common ground is the goal.
In debate, winning is the goal.

In dialogue, one listens to the other side(s) in order to understand, find meaning, and find agreement.
In debate, one listens to the other side in order to find flaws and to counter its arguments.

Dialogue enlarges and possibly changes a participant's point of view.
Debate affirms a participant's own point of view.

Dialogue reveals assumptions for reevaluation.
Debate defends assumptions as truth.

Dialogue causes introspection on one's own position.
Debate causes critique of the other position.

Dialogue opens the possibility of reaching a better solution than any of the original solutions.
Debate defends one's own positions as the best solution and excludes other solutions.

Dialogue creates an open-minded attitude: openness to being wrong and an openness to change.
Debate creates a closed-minded attitude, a determination to be right.

In dialogue, one submits one's best thinking, knowing that other people's reflections will help improve it rather than destroy it.
In debate, one submits one's best thinking and defends it against challenge to show that it is right.

Dialogue calls for temporarily suspending one's beliefs.
Debate calls for investing wholeheartedly in one's beliefs.

In dialogue, one searches for basic agreements.
In debate, one searches for glaring differences.

In dialogue, one searches for strengths in the other position.
In debate, one searches for flaws and weaknesses in the other position.

Dialogue involves a real concern for the other person and seeks to not alienate or offend.
Debate involves a countering of the other position without focusing on feelings or relationship and often belittles or deprecates the other person.

Dialogue assumes that many people have pieces of the answer and that together they can put them into a workable solution.
Debate assumes that there is a right answer and that someone has it.

Dialogue remains open-ended.
Debate implies a conclusion.

Figure 1.2 Dialogue Contrasted with Debate.

Social Workers' Participatory Action Research Readiness and Competency

Arguably, social workers are uniquely prepared for these roles—lead researcher, empowering teacher, change agent—whether alone or as leaders of interdisciplinary research and development teams. Their core preparation in clinical practice with groups, community-organizing strategies, and intervention development, implementation, and continuous improvement correspond to the competencies required for PAR leadership. For example, the lead researcher must be able to effectively select the PAR participants and then convene, organize, and mobilize them for collective action. This organizing and mobilizing work does not occur in a social vacuum. It necessitates a social setting that is conducive to group work, oftentimes one located in a welcoming, neutral, intermediary organization (Seidman, 2012).

Because diversity and manifest conflict are endemic in PAR group formations and processes, conflict mediation skills also are a practical necessity. These skills are the same ones acquired for, and associated with, clinical practice with groups. Also required are the skills and abilities related to the establishment and maintenance of prosocial norms and operational routines known to create supportive group and team climates.

Moreover, because PAR often is developed in combination with community-based participatory research, social work's community practice skills are vital. These skills start with asset-based and solution-focused community practice. They include the use of community guides, that is, residents with native knowledge and the ability to broker entry into diverse groups in various places (Kretzmann & McKnight, 1993).

What's more, these skills must include PAR-related cultural competence. Three main examples of this competence are important: (a) knowing how to proceed with inclusive and responsive PAR research questions, (b) knowing how to interpret findings regarding cultural differences without presenting them as deficits, and (c) knowing when and how to publish the research findings with special reference to the ever-present threats of language that inadvertently stereotypes, stigmatizes, and marginalizes diverse people.

Participatory Action Research as a Social Work Intervention

Democratization of the research project to include people from all walks of life opens the door to an important innovation: PAR may do "double duty" as a practice or intervention strategy (Smith & Romero, 2010). A catchy slogan introduces the main idea: "The target system also is the action system." Freely translated, this means persons identified as clients, consumers, patients, and service users, once enfranchised as co-researchers, will cogenerate the specific knowledge and interventions required to meet their own needs and solve their own problems. For example, in social work practice, PAR develops and strengthens motivational congruence between the PAR researcher and the service users, encouraging service users as co-researchers to produce the knowledge and skills they need to achieve desired outcomes (Marks, 2012). As these service users cogenerate knowledge, they also coproduce the outcomes they and the researcher-practitioner have prioritized.

On the drawing board, and ideally in practice, three good things happen at the same time. The intervention is increasingly perfected, outcomes improve, and knowledge is generated for the next practice need. When this works as planned, it is a triple-win strategy. It is enabled when social workers' training and competence for intervention design and development are brought to bear on PAR design, development, and use.

Fit for Purpose: Participatory Action Research for Specialized Problem-Solving

Every research method can be selected and evaluated in relation to a three-component criterion—fit for this purpose, in this context, and at this particular time. This same criterion can be brought to bear on PAR's rules, advantages, potential uses, and manifest limitations. The question is, What kinds of problems invite and necessitate PAR? Figure 1.3 illustrates this question. It identifies and briefly describes three kinds of problems: technical, adaptive, and wicked. Hard-and-fast distinctions between them are not important at this time. What matters are the rough-cut differences and their import for decisions regarding research designs.

Technical Problems
As indicated in Figure 1.3, technical problems can be readily defined and delimited, and evidence-based solutions are available. In intervention

Type	Certainty	Complexity	Focus/Priority	Research Agenda	Power & Authority
A Tame, Technical Problem,	*High*: The problem can be framed, named, categorized, reduced, and assigned; and the available knowledge base (including warranted interventions) is well-established	*Relatively low* with regard to the problem and the interventions; *moderate* with regard to implementation dynamics, capacity-building needs, and contextual influences	A three component agenda: (1) Ensuring a solid match between the problem(s) needing to be "solved" and the available interventions; (2) Ensuring implementation fidelity; (3) Evaluating for learning, knowledge generation, and improvement	Translational Science and Intervention Science with a focus on research-supported (evidence-based) policies and practices. Increasingly, this research is guided by formal frameworks such as Getting to Outcomes (GTO)	This research is conducted on people, organizations, communities, systems, and contexts. It is top-down and outside-in with power and authority vested squarely in the hands of expert researchers.
An Adaptive Problem	*Medium*: Although aspects of the problem can be framed and named—thanks to the existing knowledge base; novelty and ambiguity necessitate a developmental research agenda.	*High*: Although confidence about the ability to name, frame, and solve the problem endures, "there are no easy answers;" and solutions depend in part on a specially-designed, non-linear research agenda.	The first priority is a valid "theory of the problem," manifested in the ability to frame, name and categorize it. Accompanying priorities are effective solutions, paving the way for new interventions and action theories	Conceptual-operational mapping of ends-means relationships focused on good outcomes. Here, intervention-focused and problem-focused research are joined in the pursuit of new action theories	Although expert researchers and consultants retain aspects of their expert stance and personal-professional distance, adaptive problems require research <u>with</u> people, especially PAR

| A Wicked Problem | High: Although aspects of the problem can be framed, named, and categorized, overall the problem transcends conventional understanding, the current state of knowledge is inadequate, and intervention capacity and efficacy are limited. | Extraordinarily High: Doubts prevail about whether the problem can be solved in the short term, in part because the problem is home to endemic dilemmas. Researchers thus aim for manageable complexity as made via PAR, sometimes in combination with conventional scientific research.

Here, negative outcomes and lessons learned are viewed as important progress indicators because they rule out alternatives. | Empirical and theoretical advances regarding the theory of the problem constitute the top priority. This work involves simultaneous reduction/categorization of key components in the research puzzle as well as macro-level conceptual mapping of the whole, which is greater than the sum of the parts.

Developing a language system is paramount to this work because wicked problems defy ready categorization and description via the language provided by conventional theory. | Notwithstanding the import of small-scale efficacy trials and pilot studies of effectiveness, complex design and development research agendas mounted in diverse contexts and communities are the preferred strategies.

Complexity in the research is manifested in a dual focus on both single- and multi-problem interventions. The aim is to develop complex theories of change | Research teams are needed, especially for systemic participatory action research

Researchers increasingly share power and authority with laypersons, including service users. Especially when the problem is nested in community contexts, they may begin with search conferences, which are structured to clarify and help define the problem.

Researchers also typically employ community-based, participatory action research, often in combination with conventional research methods. |

Figure 1.3 Three Types of Research, Practice, and Policy Problems.

language, the theory of the problem is sufficiently comprehensive, complete, and accurate. Consequently, the main priority is to match the solution (intervention) to the defined problem. In the majority of cases where technical problems are manifest, PAR is not the best alternative. In fact, PAR's special time, capacity-building, and resource requirements may impede efficient and effective problem-solving. So, when a technical problem is evident, but research is needed, another research methodology often provides a better alternative.

Adaptive Problems

Heifetz (2006) coined the idea of an adaptive problem, and his subsequent work on adaptive leadership popularized the idea. Essentially, adaptive problems are ones for which there are no immediate and easy answers. The main reason is that the problem is not adequately defined. And this means that the research must begin with the expressed aim of problem definition and specification. Framed in intervention language, the quest is for knowledge about the theory of the problem.

PAR is an effective strategy for achieving this purpose, especially when the problem is nested in local contexts. The main assumption is that, with repeated PAR iterations, the problem will become clearer as solutions are tried and tested, iteratively and recursively, over time in often unique local contexts. From start to finish, there is a quiet confidence that the problem will be solved with time.

Wicked Problems

PAR also is an appropriate choice, perhaps the best one, when "wicked" problems must be addressed (Lawson, 2009). Wicked problems are ripe with dilemmas, so much so that they defy ready solutions. In contrast to the quiet confidence associated with adaptive problems, wicked problems are unique. There is no immediate hope that they can and will be solved. The immediate aim for all research, and especially PAR, derives from this reality. The aim is to make progress toward problem understanding via the successive piloting of potential solutions. Here, PAR provides a starting point for iterative and recursive iterations directed at gaining small wins as part of a time-consuming journey toward aspirations for huge gains.

Consider, for example, the growing concentration of multiple, co-occurring outcome and resource disparities in identifiable parts of

American cities and also in isolated, impoverished rural communities. Some analysts describe this place-based pattern as structural racism, and others describe it as structural classism (Bell & Lee, 2011). Regardless of the descriptor, the pattern is the same. Find one disparity, and you'll find others. Addressing one entails addressing the others.

Such is the nature of concentrated disadvantage (Quane & Wilson, 2012). Here, several effects nest in each other, and together they help to account for multiple outcome disparities. Specialized conventional research proceeding with just one method and focusing on one need or problem oftentimes is not fit for this purpose. In the same vein, specialized stand-alone professions, helping systems, and public policies were not developed for these circumstances and the wicked problems they breed. Presented with these vexing, potentially paralyzing, wicked problems, specially developed PAR enables progress. Two examples are noteworthy.

Example 1: Search Conference Methodology

PAR is fit for the work of gaining progressive understanding about wicked problems in special contexts. In fact, a particular kind of PAR has special import for wicked problems. It is called *search conference methodology* (Schafft & Greenwood, 2003). The main idea is to convene potential PAR researchers so that they are able to "conference" on the problem(s) needing to be addressed. "Conferencing" entails collective brainstorming structured to begin mapping new conceptual territory. A brief description follows, starting with an important contrast with research.

When entirely new problems must be addressed, and they are not understood, "the search" precedes research. "Re-search" involves replication and extension studies. It is a repeat performance whereby investigators seek knowledge via methods that have gamelike structures and rules. Significantly, it proceeds in relation to conceptual territory that already has been mapped. Where wicked problems prevail, an important question looms: What is to be done when no such conceptual mapping has been completed?

Search conference methodology is one response. It sets the stage for research as participants map what once was uncharted territory. The reminder here is that a scientific and scholarly search nearly always precedes re-search, especially when the scientific method is employed. The main reason is that science depends on and articulates theory. So, the conceptual territory must be mapped, if only in a preliminary way, before the investigative game and its methodological rule structures can be determined and implemented.

PAR search conference methodology is structured to do this mapping. It is directed toward the outline of a feasible theory of the problem. The immediate aim is to transform potentially paralyzing uncertainty and novelty into manageable complexity. It depends on agreements regarding the framing and defining of the problem, as well as the language systems that should be used. Once this theoretical mapping has occurred, that is, PAR is directed toward the theory of the problem on the drawing board, PAR can commence strategically and efficiently as problem-solving in real-world contexts.

Example 2: Participatory Action Research for Complex Cross-System Change

Especially where wicked problems prevail, specialized professions, stand-alone organizations, and separate policy sectors need to be connected, harmonized, and synchronized, starting with agreements on common purposes. Three main descriptors increasingly are used to describe this agenda: (a) interprofessional collaboration, (b) interorganizational partnerships, and (c) policy integration (Lawson, 2009; 2013). The ideal is to develop a mutually beneficial synergy involving, for example, education, mental health, child welfare, health, juvenile justice, domestic violence, substance abuse, and workforce development. In the process, industrial age professions, organizations, and social institutions are reconfigured for 21st-century global societies.

Clearly, this agenda is center stage in social work's missions for today's fast-changing world. For example, in many parts of the United States, work is under way to unite all public sector systems around a shared agenda. This agenda is to develop trauma-informed systems, encompassing all affected professions and organizations (Caringi & Lawson, under review).

Essentially, a trauma-informed system is a formal set of roles, rules, responsibilities, and relationships for addressing two kinds of trauma adversity: (1) primary and (2) secondary. An example of the first kind is compelling research about the short- and long-term consequences of adverse childhood experiences (e.g., Anda, Butchart, Felitti, & Brown,

2010). Another example is the persistent trauma of military veterans who have experienced horrific life experiences.

It is not unusual for the human services professionals who work with people affected by primary trauma to experience personal, vicarious traumatization. The official descriptor is secondary traumatic stress (STS), and it is a new priority in the public sector workforces in education, child welfare, mental health, juvenile justice, and so forth (Caringi, Lawson, & Devlin, 2012). STS exacts its own tolls, including persistent anxiety, inability to sleep, depression and perhaps substance abuse to cope with these other presenting systems. It also is instrumental in workforce problems, starting with undesirable turnover.

The work of developing trauma-informed systems, in short, can be framed as an especially complex adaptive problem, and probably a wicked one. The question is, How best can social workers, professionals from other disciplines, and public policymakers begin to address this daunting complexity?

Pioneering work in the United Kingdom provides an important resource—a new PAR methodology. Burns (2010) provides details about this new methodology. He calls it "systemic action research." On close inspection, it is PAR involving multiple sectors and each sector's representative actors. For example, each participating organization (e.g., a school system, a mental health system, a child welfare system) has its PAR team. Additionally, there is a cross-system leadership team, and it is structured to coordinate, align, and provide leadership for each organization's team. In this fashion, knowledge about complex systems change is gained as the actual work of systems change commences and proceeds. Knowledge for systems change practice is progressively derived from complex PAR as system change practice. Such is one way to address the problem of designing, implementing, and improving trauma-informed systems.

Comparable work, led by social workers, has been completed in the United States—and with an important, unique addition. This work involves cross-system service integration to address co-occurring and interacting needs. The main needs addressed are substance abuse, mental health needs (especially depression), domestic violence, and employment challenges, including unemployment and underemployment. This work proceeded with PAR design teams (Anderson-Butcher, Lawson, & Barkdull, 2003; Lawson, Anderson-Butcher, Petersen, & Barkdull, 2003). Like Burns's

(2010) designs for systemic action research, it involved a cross-system coordinative team with oversight over the design teams working in four states. In addition to the priorities for interprofessional collaboration, interorganizational partnerships, and policy integration, this systemic participatory action research involving design teams had another keynote feature. Service users, or "clients," were viewed as experts and added to the PAR design teams. In other words, in addition to interprofessional collaboration, these PAR teams proceeded with service user collaboration.

The evaluations of this systems change agenda reveal the importance of the current and former clients' expertise in knowledge development and progressive systems change. In fact, the social workers and other helping professionals on these PAR design teams identified collaboration with clients as the most important stimulus for systems change. What's more, local agencies hired these current and former clients to assist with services planning, implementation, and improvement because professionals learned how much they did not know—and also how much expertise these services users had to offer.

The knowledge and practice innovations gained from this complex PAR would not have happened without an experimental mind-set on the part of this initiative's designers. Their experimental mind-set included the willingness to assume the risks associated with teams consisting of expert professionals and laypeople, called service users and clients. None of the resultant benefits would have been reaped with a conventional research design.

Toward Theories of Action and Theories of Change

Finally, just as conventional science is structured to articulate theory (descriptive-explanatory theory), PAR is structured to develop and articulate theory, albeit a unique and important kind of theory: PAR is designed to contribute to theories of, and for, action, also known as action theories or theories of change (e.g., Fullbright-Anderson & Auspos, 2006; Philliber, 1998; Preskill & Beer, 2012). Action theories for social change are a special priority for some researchers, and they have developed special partnership configurations to achieve this aim (St. John, 2013). These action theories, by whatever name, are structured by cause-and-effect propositions. In conventional descriptive-explanatory theories, these propositions are manifest in "if this, then that" statements and "when this, then that" statements. Action theories, or theories of change, also are structured by propositions, albeit action-oriented ones. For example, "When this, do that" and "If that, do this." Together, these propositions define operational pathways toward the achievement of desirable outcomes, and they are part and parcel of PAR-driven efforts to develop valid, reliable, and useful knowledge.

Admittedly futuristic in today's social work and other helping professions, the conditions are ripe for the articulation of descriptive-explanatory theories. In brief, everyone now confronts outcome-based (results-oriented) accountability systems. To the extent that empirically grounded theories of action for practice and policy can be developed and refined, professions and the people they serve will be mutually advantaged. PAR's unique qualities and contributions to these action-oriented theories recommend its inclusion in research initiatives.

COMPARING AND CONTRASTING PARTICIPATORY ACTION RESEARCH WITH CONVENTIONAL RESEARCH

The analysis so far recommends PAR as a formal research methodology. After all, research is a formal process by which investigators systematically study an important phenomenon. It is called the phenomenon of interest, and research is structured to generate knowledge about it. PAR, as described above, does exactly that, albeit in an unusual way: knowledge is gained as real-world problem-solving proceeds. What, then, are some of the key differences between PAR and conventional research?

A Different Relationship Between the Researcher and the Participants

Rooted in the Enlightenment, with its tensions and conflicts with religion and tradition, there is a conventional approach to scientific research, and graduate research methods classes in nearly every academic discipline are structured to disseminate it. This dominant approach or paradigm (Kuhn, 1996) has an understandable, predictable, and justifiable rationale and rule structure, and it can be introduced in the following way. This approach entails social distancing to enhance objectivity and impartiality, while at the same time preventing and eliminating personal opinions and biases as well as all manner of doctrines (e.g., religious, organizational, institutional). Expressed in colloquial terms, the aim can be summarized as follows: Don't get too close to the people and the problem you're investigating, because interpersonal ties and preconceived ideas about your research problem will jeopardize your investigation. If these biases prevail, they will influence your study and will cast doubt on the truth values, reliability, and use values of the knowledge you claim to have generated.

These several assumptions are consequential for how research is structured and conducted. Oftentimes, this kind of research is characterized as *observational research*. Its rule structure follows suit. The investigator is required to self-consciously impose personal distance from the people, the research problem, and the research context.

This kind of observational research is known colloquially as "spectator research" because the investigator, in order to produce valid and reliable knowledge, must be divorced from the action as the investigator watches and collects data. Toward this end, the rules of the scientific game are structured to prevent the researcher from becoming immersed in the action and developing prejudicial connections with the actors being studied. Clearly, PAR marks a radical departure from this social distancing between the researcher and the participants.

The Origin of the Research Question

One way to safeguard conventional research and the researcher from bias is to provide rules for determining the research question. In conventional scientific research, the question originates in one or more theories (Kuhn, 1996). Put differently, researchers look to the theory they wish to test for their research question. The rationale is straightforward: The purpose of scientific research is to articulate theory, and the only surefire way to do this is by deriving the research question from the preferred theory.

Although the research question for PAR may emanate from theory and involve theory testing, PAR questions are derived mainly from two sources. They emanate from practice and policy and also from the need to address urgent needs and solve pressing problems in real-world contexts. Significantly, laypeople have the requisite power and authority to introduce and define the question.

Designated Researcher Roles and Relationships

Observational research, the rule-driven distancing of the researcher from the actors and actions being investigated, is framed by a formal system for knowledge generation. In fact, the dominant view of research is embedded in a social system designed to make research-based knowledge valid, reliable, and useful. Like all manner of systems, this one has formal rules, roles, relationships, and responsibilities.

Specifically, there are basic or pure researchers, also called "bench researchers" in the natural and biological sciences. These researchers generate new theories and knowledge without an immediate priority for application and use values. Oftentimes motivated by curiosity, they pursue knowledge for its own sake. In the academic world, this pursuit of knowledge may be characterized as "free intelligence" and "academic freedom."

In addition to basic or pure researchers, this system also has roles and responsibilities for applied researchers. Intervention researchers typically are included in this group. In the main, these applied researchers draw on and apply the work of basic and pure researchers in the pursuit of improved results in the real world. Sometimes these applied researchers' work is viewed as translational, that is, their aim is to move the research agenda from the scientific bench to the practice and policy trenches (Kerner & Hall, 2009). In other instances—especially in some kinds of intervention research (Rothman & Thomas, 2009)—applied research is framed and conducted with no reliance on basic research. Either way, these applied researchers are interested in actionable, useful knowledge for practice and policy. Toward this end, some design *efficacy trials*. Here, they strive to achieve hypothesized and desired results under controlled, laboratory-like experimental situations.

Building on the results of efficacy trials, these applied investigators then move to real-world settings with *effectiveness research*, sometimes called practice research. Although this effectiveness research often is preceded by efficacy trials, it also is the case that efficacy trials are bypassed in the interest of time and real-world effectiveness.

The social system for research and progressive knowledge generation, application, dissemination, and use is founded on the scientific method's priorities for a sufficient number of replication and extension studies (Kuhn, 1996). These studies are like consumer product warranties because the "knowledge warrants" for research are both a priority and a protection for research users and consumers. The greater the number of studies with convergent findings, the better the knowledge warrants.

In conventional or "normal" science, two other main assumptions are noteworthy. First, a sufficient number of high-quality replication and extension studies are needed in order for the knowledge they yield and the theory they articulate to have warranted truth and use values. The second major assumption follows suit: When this theoretical, research-based knowledge has warranted truth, reliability, and use values, its generalizability (and transportability) from people to people and place to place is enhanced.

In brief, this research system has a clear-cut division of labor, which helps to account for its special constitutive and regulative rules. Research specialists are needed for basic (pure) research, and other specialists are needed for applied research. Although some people may perform both roles, in today's era of increasing specialization, researchers must make choices. For example, some basic researchers prefer not to be involved in real-world practice, yet others would not have it any other way.

Knowledge Must Travel, and It Takes Time

There is another reason why a division of labor is center stage in the conventional research system—knowledge must travel from basic researchers to applied researchers, and still later, from applied researchers to practitioners, policy makers, and lay knowledge consumers. The conventional system depends in part on solid relationships among researchers. It also hinges on the mechanisms for knowledge transfers and handoffs.

Knowledge travels in two ways. One is through formal dissemination mechanisms (e.g., university courses, formal training; reviews of research). The other way is by informal diffusion channels such as practitioner networks (Dearing, 2009; Kerner & Hall, 2009). Either way, it takes time to get knowledge into action.

Last but not least, knowledge generation and use are either facilitated or constrained by the preferred research-to-practice-and-policy strategy. The main question is worth pondering. Is the strategy formal dissemination (e.g., research briefs, formal training courses), diffusion through less formal channels and networks, or some combination of both? Regardless of the answer, all of this takes time. And time is a precious resource because people's lives and the destinies of organizations and places often require urgent, strategic, and effective action.

In conventional research, time is a precious resource in another way. It takes time to complete a sufficient number of replication and extension studies, whether as efficacy trials or effectiveness research. For better or worse, one consequence of this system is that it often takes years, even decades, for conventional research to generate the kinds of valid, reliable, and useful knowledge needed for optimal policy and practice.

There is no escape from this requirement. The scientific investigative process simply cannot be rushed, because of the dire consequences of prematurely claiming knowledge validity, reliability, certainty, predictability, and use values. A firm reminder is especially relevant here. Underdeveloped and flawed knowledge in the hands of naïve and unskilled users has the potential to cause harm in the name of doing good work.

Participation in Conventional Research

Clear roles and relationships with firm boundaries are manifest in conventional, dominant research approaches. Formally trained and credentialed scientists and scholars are the researchers. Only peers with identical and comparable specialized training and expertise are able to participate in the investigative game, judge how it is played, and evaluate the knowledge gained from the investigation. This exclusive view influences laypeople's roles and researchers' relationships with them.

In principle and in practice, conventional research is founded on a nonnegotiable rule: Laypeople lack the expertise to participate in the design, conduct, and publication of research. This rule means that nonresearchers have two roles. Laypersons, practitioners, and policymakers are research participants (or subjects), and they are research consumers and users.

Beyond these role descriptions are power and authority relationships. Specialist researchers and scholars are the authorities. They know what laypeople do not. To the extent that these specialists have knowledge that laypeople and policymakers need and want, investigators also have special power. They know what others need to know and do. Critics of this knowledge-as-power hierarchy criticize the unequal relations it structures and maintains. At the same time, they emphasize PAR's comparative advantages. To reiterate, PAR democratizes relationships among all research participants, thus corresponding to citizens' civic engagement in democratic political structures and operational processes.

CONCLUDING THOUGHTS

The preceding analysis, especially the comparisons and contrasts involving PAR and conventional research, highlights the importance of research alternatives and the choices they involve. As social work and all other helping professions struggle to keep pace with dramatic, rapid societal change, enduring questions about research gain new currency and meaning.

Even if readers are not attracted to PAR methodology, the questions it raises are ones that merit their deliberation: Which research questions matter the most? Whose questions matter? Where do these questions originate? How and from whom will practitioners and policy makers get valid, reliable, useful, and trustworthy knowledge for their work? How long will it take to get this knowledge to them? In turn, what and whose knowledge counts, and under what circumstances, when, and why? Last, but not least, whose interests are served by the answers to these questions, and what goals and objectives are connected to these interests? Which ones are omitted when these interests dominate?

Together, these grand questions enable the evaluation of every field's research system. Framed and evaluated as a research system, new avenues open for its strategic redefinition and expansion. PAR, as presented in this and succeeding chapters, can be viewed in this way. It opens new avenues for planning, evaluating, and improving a helping profession's research system. Which methods are acceptable, and which ones are not?

This analysis indicates that the answer to this question need not amount to a zero-sum game, because every research method is selective. Every method, therefore, produces limited knowledge and understanding even as it yields important new knowledge and understanding. In

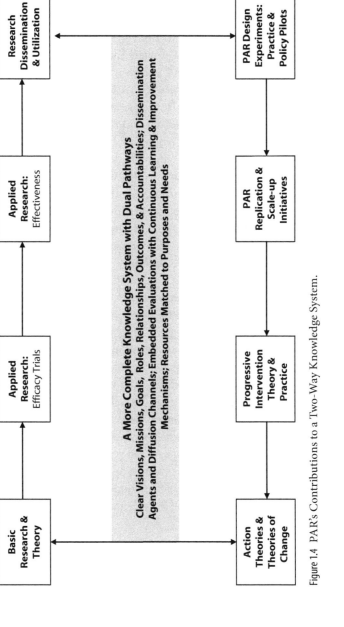

Figure 1.4 PAR's Contributions to a Two-Way Knowledge System.

this view, PAR is a viable, unique, and critically important alternative, either alone or in combination with other research methods. Toward this end, PAR's main assumptions have been identified. Its rules and special features have been described and explained. The adaptive and wicked problems for which it is suited have been presented at the same time that PAR's limitations with technical problems have been identified.

Moreover, differences in PAR design and practice have been presented, and so have differences between PAR and conventional scientific research. These differences are consequential for everyone interested in the relationship between research and the common good—locally, regionally, nationally, and internationally.

Today's dominant research mode can be described with a familiar metaphor: "Theory and research must travel from the scientific bench to the trenches of policy and practice, and it must be translated and applied along the way." In this dominant view, the research-and-practice relationship is basically a one-way street. Granting its multiple benefits, this knowledge travel takes time, and it entails a host of related requirements. It often falls short of expectations.

From this perspective, PAR can be illuminated and appreciated anew. It opens up avenues for a two-way knowledge street because it is rooted in practice and real-world policy contexts, and it is cogenerated by scholar change agents who organize, mobilize, and strive to empower groups of people—it starts in the practice and policy trenches.

Figure 1.4 depicts this expanded knowledge system. It emphasizes dual knowledge pathways, together with opportunities for mutually beneficial research and knowledge interchanges. Here, PAR opens avenues for knowledge development described as "from the practice and policy trenches to the academic benches where action theories and theories of action can be formulated and progressively tested." Viewed in this way, PAR can inform the work of applied researchers and basic researchers. Science in service of humankind is advanced when such complementary relationships are in evidence.

2

Child Welfare Participatory Action Research Design Teams for Workforce Reconfiguration, Organizational Innovation, and Policy Change

Hal A. Lawson and James C. Caringi

INTRODUCTION

The aim for this chapter is to introduce, describe, and explain a particular model for systems change in child welfare. It is called a design team model, and it is defined by the participatory action research (PAR) that team members undertake with competent team facilitation. The design metaphor is apt and important because teams are charged with two related kinds of creative work: (a) the redesign of existing workforce arrangements, organizational structures, and operational procedures; and (b) the creation of entirely new designs, ones that move beyond mere reforms to organizational and policy transformations.

Why structure a team, charging them with responsibilities for redesign and design? A dual rationale provides one answer. First, team-driven redesign and design innovations are needed to achieve desired results for vulnerable children, youth, and families at scale. Second, these results will not be achieved systematically and sustainably until workforce outcomes improve. These latter outcomes start with desirable retention and the prevention of undesirable turnover, and they include workforce development systems that enable organizational learning, knowledge generation, and continuous quality improvement.

THE DEVELOPMENT OF THE DESIGN TEAM IDEA

The idea of organizations with their own design teams has a distinguished history on both sides of the Atlantic. In the United States, Kurt Lewin (1951), his students, and other American organizational development specialists pioneered this approach. The equivalent in Great Britain started with the Tavistock Institute and featured the pioneering work of Fred Emery and Eric Trist. Together these transatlantic initiatives spawned a particular school of thought and a specialized practice with an international reach.

In action research circles, three revealing names announce this special PAR approach. It became known as "the northern tradition" because at one time it was exclusively practiced in the global north. It also became known as "organizational action research," a label that has differentiated it from community-based PAR. The third name, "workplace democracy," derived from the fact that a PAR design team enables front-line workers to enjoy voice and choice as they generate knowledge about how to solve organizational problems and meet their own needs.

Public sector bureaucracies characterized by top-down, compliance-oriented, and sometimes punitive leadership, management, and supervision are special candidates for PAR design teams. Bureaucracies that get sidetracked, essentially ignoring and neglecting results for their client system and also the needs of their workforce, are special candidates. Lipsky's (1980) rationale is central to this work. Impersonal bureaucracies that emphasize self-serving "people-processing routines" at the expense of "people-changing technologies" are prime targets. Service users are the losers when this people-processing pattern prevails. For example, the social worker is able to claim, "I provided the required services, but my clients refused to adhere, comply, and change." Or, in the case of the public school teacher, "I taught them, but they refused to learn."

Clearly, goal displacement is manifest here. That is, practices originally designed to achieve outcomes for clients and students—as strategies to achieve client goals—have become the new goals—as indicated above in the cases of the teacher and the social worker. Flaws and errors flourish under these conditions. In fact, public servants charged with doing good may inadvertently cause harm, especially when there are no checks and balances to detect and correct these problems (Allen-Scott, Hatfield, & McIntyre, 2014).

INTRODUCING PARTICIPATORY ACTION RESEARCH DESIGN TEAMS

To prevent and address this suboptimal state of affairs and to improve service design and delivery, organizational and interorganizational PAR design teams have been developed and tested (Anderson-Butcher, Lawson, & Barkull, 2003; Caringi et al., 2008; Claiborne & Lawson, 2011). Because these PAR design teams are problem-solving mechanisms, they can be viewed as interventions, albeit a special kind. These teams are special because they generate knowledge and articulate theory as they address practical problems. As this chapter's title announces, these teams' improvement targets include new workforce configurations, organizational innovations, and even public policy change.

Public child welfare systems have manifest needs for this special PAR design team intervention. After examples of these special needs are provided, the team facilitator's role and responsibilities are outlined, and examples of practical team tools are provided. Examples of team-generated improvements and innovations follow. Finally, evidence in support of team effectiveness is summarized briefly, paving the way for a sample of team start-up and facilitation "lessons learned."

CHILD WELFARE SYSTEMS AND PARTICIPATORY ACTION RESEARCH DESIGN TEAMS

Public child welfare systems are assigned a daunting, critically important responsibility—protecting and supporting vulnerable children. To achieve this aim, organizations typically configure their workforce to enable some degree of specialization. Two kinds of specialists are especially noteworthy. Child protection services specialists respond to allegations and documented incidents involving child abuse and neglect, oftentimes in partnership with police officers. Their protective services work becomes more complicated and dangerous when these workers must respond to families located in isolated rural communities and high-poverty urban neighborhoods challenged by crime, structural racism, and social isolation (Sampson, 2012). Ultimately, these child protective services workers share responsibility with specialists in the justice system for decisions about whether to remove children from their homes.

Foster care specialists pick up where child protection ends. Foster care workers strive to ensure that children in governmental custody are placed in safe, health-enhancing family systems and enjoy the assistance, social supports, and resources they need to develop into productive citizens. These specialists are asked to do an unusual amount of boundary crossing, because kids in foster care often are clients in several systems—mental health, special education, public health, and perhaps juvenile justice.

Foster care specialists' work is less dangerous than that of child protective services workers. However, foster care practice is inherently stressful, because the children in foster care have been abused and neglected, and their foster parents may not be ready for their social/emotional needs and behavior. Predictably, foster care specialists routinely are asked to help foster parents cope with and respond to these kids' needs, and they also are charged with finding a new family placement when the initial one does not work out. Understandably, the challenges mount with each new placement because the children are increasingly destabilized. Children involved in these transitions understandably act out.

More Than a Technical Problem: Adaptive Challenges

Clearly, both child protection and foster care workers share several important features. To begin with, both specializations are stressful and oftentimes dangerous. More than a technical set of tasks, this work entails addressing adaptive problems. Moreover, this work is inherently and deeply emotional. The emotional labor of these workers needs to be monitored, and secondary traumatic stress prevention and early intervention is a never-ending priority (Caringi, Lawson, & Devlin, 2012; Caringi & Hardiman, 2011).

Moreover, both child protection and foster care work depend on a unique kind of specialization that requires extraordinary breadth and depth of knowledge as well as the ability to translate that knowledge into demonstrated practice competence. In fact, the case can be made that social work credentials, indeed a social work master's degree, should be mandatory for both child protection and foster care certification. At one time, this specialized social work training and certification were required in the majority of states. This is not the case today.

In many states, today's norm is a mixed workforce consisting of official social workers and others with little or no social work training. Paradoxically, these other workers tend to be called, and often call themselves, social workers. The result, using social work terms, is that the child welfare workforce has become deprofessionalized. This means that some rural agencies and huge urban systems enjoy the services of few, if any, officially prepared and licensed social workers. Public child welfare workforces are described accordingly as "mixed" because they have varying combinations of official social workers and workers without official social work training and degrees.

The overall situation is far from ideal. Workers without social work degrees often are overmatched in relation to de facto work role demands and responsibilities. Meanwhile, the civil service system provides no special roles and privileges for official social workers, and these same workers often search in vain for a supportive professional culture. Predictably, both kinds of workers tend to exit the system as better opportunities arise, so much so that turnover has reached epidemic levels (Strolin-Goltzman et al., 2009).

Not all such turnover is undesirable. However, when child welfare agencies become something akin to "workforce revolving doors," adverse effects follow. For example, when turnover is high, children, youth, and families are not provided with consistent, stable, quality care. At the same time, top-level leaders, managers, supervisors, and agency trainers must constantly attend to the induction, deployment, and preparation of new workers.

Significantly, front-line workers in every department typically are asked to fill in for departed workers, oftentimes on top of already heavy caseloads, resulting in their making their own plans to leave the agency. Under these conditions, the aforementioned people-processing routines typically trump people-changing technologies (Lipsky, 1980). People processing is especially likely when system leaders require scripted practices because they worry about the adverse effects of a child's death or a horrendous incident in which the agency is blamed and threatened with a lawsuit. What is more, blame and maltreatment cycles develop and flourish under these circumstances, ultimately having a negative impact on organizational climate (a here-and-now state of affairs, which, like the weather, can change). When these cycles endure, organizational culture also is influenced negatively, that is, the agency's historical trajectory, traditions, and values are affected (Glisson & Hemmelgarn, 1998).

Introducing Participatory Action Research Design Teams

To reiterate, PAR design teams are workforce, organizational, and policy interventions. Their primary purpose is to optimize the conditions needed to achieve desirable results for children, youth, and families and, at the same time, to optimize workforce configurations, organizational designs, and public policies. Again, the main assumption is that workforce characteristics and outcomes are the most important determinants of outcomes for children, families, and communities.

Once design teams are viewed and developed as interventions, interest turns to the targets for these interventions. Where workforce issues are concerned, the organization is the primary target, and so PAR teams are structured with appropriate representation to impact their respective organizations. Because people and organizations experiencing turmoil cannot be expected to pull themselves up by their own bootstraps and form a highly effective team, external team facilitation is a basic requirement.

Formation and Characteristics of Design Teams

Design teams represent the various roles, informal cliques, and networks in the agency. They range in size from 8 to 25 persons. Local leadership, sometimes in consultation with representative workers, determines the team's exact size and composition. Some members are appointed, and others are elected. Team selection procedures vary by the agency.

In the beginning, a specially prepared outside facilitator orchestrates the design teams. The facilitator's job is to help a group of diverse, representative employees become a productive, healthy team. Social work's group practice skills are a mainstay in this team development. Facilitators must attend to two aspects of team development. The *social side* of team development, which refers to the process by which a loosely connected group becomes a true team, must be balanced with the *task side,* which refers to problem-solving and knowledge development. Figure 2.1 provides an overview.

What the Design Team Does

Design teams are tasked with figuring out the causes of organizational and workforce problems such as undesirable turnover. The teams also are charged with developing workforce and organizational improvements that will increase desirable retention, ultimately leading to better services and improved results. Consistent with the idea of a true team, members depend on one another as they figure out the problems and craft intervention solutions.

For example, team members get feedback from co-workers about remedies for undesirable turnover and for improvements needed for retention. Teams also are responsible for ensuring that co-workers support improvements and "spread the good news" when innovations are developed. In these ways, a team acts as an "agency nerve center." Figure 2.2 provides an overview.

Team members need both individual and collective will and skill to succeed. Trained facilitators help provide these skills as they strive to help build team competence and sustainability. For example, facilitators help team members appreciate the need for ongoing data collection, data-informed decision-making, and continual feedback from others in the organization.

Accurate, "actionable" data are especially important. Structured and operating in this way, teams can be viewed as integrated problem-solving, knowledge generation, and organizational learning mechanisms. Significantly, this design team approach is decidedly strengths based

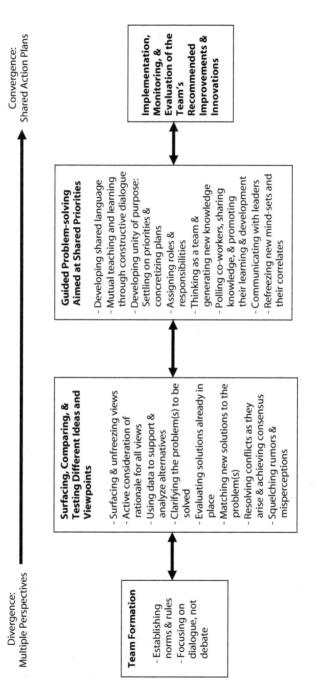

Divergence:
Multiple Perspectives

Convergence:
Shared Action Plans

Team Formation

- Establishing norms & rules
- Focusing on dialogue, not debate

Surfacing, Comparing, & Testing Different Ideas and Viewpoints

- Surfacing & unfreezing views
- Active consideration of rationale for all views
- Using data to support & analyze alternatives
- Clarifying the problem(s) to be solved
- Evaluating solutions already in place
- Matching new solutions to the problem(s)
- Resolving conflicts as they arise & achieving consensus
- Squelching rumors & misperceptions

Guided Problem-solving Aimed at Shared Priorities

- Developing shared language
- Mutual teaching and learning through constructive dialogue
- Developing unity of purpose: Settling on priorities & concretizing plans
- Assigning roles & responsibilities
- Thinking as a team & generating new knowledge
- Polling co-workers, sharing knowledge, & promoting their learning & development
- Communicating with leaders
- Refreezing new mind-sets and their correlates

Implementation, Monitoring, & Evaluation of the Team's Recommended Improvements & Innovations

Figure 2.1 A Developmental Progression for Team Formation, Functioning, and Action Planning.

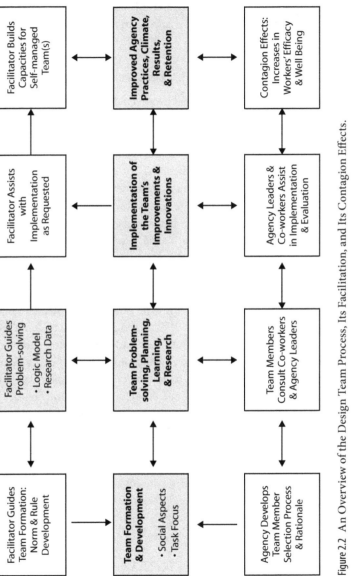

Figure 2.2 An Overview of the Design Team Process, Its Facilitation, and Its Contagion Effects.

and solution focused. Suitably facilitated teams send the metamessage that workers are valued, helping to create a positive team culture and overall organizational climate, especially as teams make progress in solving problems that influence everyone in the organization.

Teams, Other Agency Staff, and Top-Level Leaders Working Together

Teams structured in suboptimal work environments cannot do this problem-solving work alone. In the near term, every troubled organization and a start-up team need outside help provided by a facilitator. The facilitator is responsible for helping agency members initiate several related improvements—simultaneously. For example, teams help agencies open up new lines of communication, develop new problem-solving resources and supports, generate new knowledge about retention and child welfare practice, and shift leadership, management, and supervision to a more participatory-democratic style (Claiborne & Lawson, 2011).

This new leadership, management, and supervisory style is especially important. It entails "*doing with*" rather than "*doing to*" workers, and it is based on the belief that each worker has expertise that needs to be tapped. This new philosophy and leadership style draws on the theory and practice of participatory democracy. Workplace democracy, in combination with workers' increasing commitments and engagement, promises to enhance the agency's culture and climate, ultimately improving desirable retention and, later, giving rise to better practices and policies that are instrumental in achieving better outcomes for children and families.

Although an outside facilitator is needed at start-up, the plan is for teams to become self-directed and self-sustaining. For this to occur, the facilitator needs to be involved in capacity-building, especially as teams are formed. Mirroring clinical and direct practice with individuals, facilitators should also have a firm plan for their own disengagement, a plan designed to yield member empowerment and team sustainability.

FACILITATING THE DEVELOPMENT OF A TRUE TEAM

Teams are collective structures for PAR. Specially prepared and supported social workers typically have served as PAR team facilitators.

Social workers are recommended in many organizations because they bring an important combination of clinical and direct practice competencies, group practice skills, and organizational development expertise. These three kinds of expertise are essential because team facilitators routinely face three interacting team development and performance challenges—micro (direct practice with individuals), meso (group skills), and macro (organizational development and policy change competence).

As mentioned previously, design teams consist of diverse, representative people from the agency who often have little or no prior history of working together effectively and successfully. In fact, some members come to the team with prior histories involving finger-pointing, blaming dynamics, counterproductive conflict, and even hostility. Although some conflict can be harnessed for constructive problem-solving, negative conflicts and raw emotions have the potential to derail team development and performance. In high-turnover agencies, these conflicts and emotions are ready to erupt at any time. The facilitator is charged to keep them in check, indeed, to use them as opportunities for consensus development, innovation, and improvement.

In fact, teams tend to be microcosms of the overall agency. In both teams and agencies, some people do not treat each other nicely and appropriately. This suboptimal quality of treatment and interaction problem tends to foul the agency's culture and climate, and left unchecked, it has the same effect in design teams. Workers leave in part because of this quality of treatment and interaction problem. In the same vein, members will leave the team unless the facilitator prevents interactions characterized by blame and maltreatment dynamics.

In short, absent skilled facilitation, members will act like a hastily convened group rather than a true team (Hackman, 2012). In a true team, all members are interdependent, and they build healthy relationships as they solve important retention-related problems. Even with skilled facilitation, the development of a true team may be challenging. Challenges are especially likely when conflicts and unhealthy dynamics from outside the team are allowed to intrude into team formation and problem-solving. The facilitator's job is to prevent these conflicts and unhealthy dynamics, and also to intervene early when they present themselves.

Of course, a facilitator cannot do all of this work alone. The team needs every team member to share responsibility and accountability for positive, productive relationships and interactions. One key strategy is to insist on strengths-based, solution-focused, and blame-free language. Every team member needs to pledge to use this language, and to remind others to do the same. Another strategy is to insist on dialogue instead of debate, as discussed in chapter 1.

In this light, team facilitators, as well as all PAR investigators, need to take stock of Tuckman & Jensen's (1977) research on group formation and performance. Their research yielded a four-phase developmental process. After a group *forms*, it experiences emotional *storms*. These storms give rise to consensual *norms*, without which the group cannot *perform*. Drawing on this research, team facilitation starts with norm formation, followed by rules and operational procedures. The idea is to prevent harmful, interpersonal storms, especially ones that derail team development. Figure 2.3 provides an example of team operational guidelines. Figure 2.4 identifies team member roles and responsibilities.

Toward this end, several practical tools have been field-tested for design teams (Lawson & Caringi, 2008). These same tools are directly applicable to all manner of PAR initiatives because the same worries about harmful storms surround their formation and progressive development.

Together, these team tools are provided to optimize the conditions for authentic teams (Hackman, 2012). Focused on the social side of team formation and performance, they also influence the task side (i.e., the actual problem-solving work teams undertake). PAR via teams fundamentally depends on tools like these. These tools' import is especially evident when storms resurface (i.e., when "hot button" problems evoke long-standing conflicts).

Not all such conflict is problematic, and some of it cannot be avoided or prevented. Conflict is endemic in teams because they are the "troubled agency" in miniature. As members learn how to rely on these kinds of tools and develop into a productive team with a positive climate, the aim is for these tools and the PAR process to spill over into every aspect of the agency. Put differently, starting with their progressive development and especially when authentic PAR teams have been formed, "contagion effects" and "ripple effects" are prioritized (see Figure 2.2).

Some teams, never arrive at this ideal state, in part because team members are unable to get beyond long-standing stereotypes, pet peeves, and adverse relationships. Even so, a design team can be a productive

1. At the beginning of each meeting, the training team facilitator and team members will:
   - Clearly state and agree on the purpose of the meeting
   - Review progress and achievements from previous meetings as reflected in the written summary prepared by the training facilitator
2. Agree to focus on problem-solving dialogue, while avoiding potentially damaging debates (refer to companion guidelines)
3. Recognize that conflict and diversity are assets to be maximized, not problems needing to be avoided and suppressed, and develop conflict resolution procedures.
4. Agree on procedures that ensure that every voice is heard and that the problem-solving dialogue is focused, detailed, and productive. For example:
   - Avoid long speeches by asking each person to identify and describe briefly just one problem, need, improvement strategy, or obstacle
   - Use round robin strategies to ensure that everyone has the opportunity to offer perspectives on, and ask questions about, this problem, need, strategy, or obstacle
   - Develop a logic model, including the specific need or problem; its causes; desirable solutions; and anticipated results and benefits
   - Reach preliminary consensus on the likely facilitators, constraints, obstacles, and barriers for improvements (e.g., co-workers lack certain competencies)
   - Identify barrier-busting and problem-solving mechanisms (e.g., design and deliver training that develops co-workers' competencies)
5. Agree on "a parking lot" for ideas that are not immediately relevant and useful; and revisit the parking lot during the debriefing process (see the companion guideline below).
6. Do not "lump together" too many needs, problems, and priorities so that you end up with an unmanageable problem.
7. Because the team may have to make some hard choices, develop a prioritizing process that is acceptable to all members. For example, agree on a method for selecting the five most important identified areas of improvement (e.g., voting with "stickies" and "dots"); and then put the remaining issues in the "issue and idea parking lot."
8. "Chunk" out action steps as often as possible in CONCRETE ways that demonstrate to the team and others that progress is being made. Do this as early in the process as possible to help get some momentum going for the team.
9. Develop an orientation/mentoring process for members joining late in the process and for members who miss a meeting. For example, develop a "buddy" system where 2-3 members take someone new to lunch a week or so before the meeting, provide them with copies of materials, and try to bring them up to speed as much as possible to avoid taking valuable time in the meetings going back to square one.
10. At the midpoint of each meeting, the team facilitator will do process, progress, and product checks, helping to ensure that the problem-solving dialogue and interactions are healthy and productive.
11. At the end of each meeting, the team facilitator and team members will debrief, summarizing progress, achievements, and barriers; celebrating successes; and identifying next steps.
12. Also at the end of each meeting, the team will decide what information can be shared agency-wide, including who on the team will share this information with top level leadership.

Figure 2.3 Team Operational Guidelines.

Shape the Agenda: Solicit co-workers' views of recruitment needs and retention problems and share this information with the team.

Contribute to Team Formation and Functioning: Identify and help enforce shared norms, rules, and operational guidelines; welcome and help orient new members; help pick up the slack when someone leaves or needs help; and follow through on assignments.

Engage in the Design Team Process: Attend every team meeting, come prepared, build trust among team members, do not withhold important information, listen actively to other members' views, participate in problem-solving dialogue aimed at consensus.

Search for Relationships and Root Causes: When it's possible to do so, identify patterns involving recruitment needs and retention problems and pinpoint their primary causes.

Focus on Solutions: Identify improvement models and strategies that respond to needs, solve problems, and build on individual, group, and organizational strengths.

Identify Constraints, Obstacles, and Barriers: Identify the factors and forces that limit, inhibit, and prevent effective improvement strategies and promising innovations.

Develop Barrier-Busting Strategies: Identify people, resources, strategies, and models that reduce, eliminate, and prevent problematic constraints, obstacles, and barriers.

Request Training and Learning Resources: Enlist the team facilitator's assistance in providing responsive training and mobilizing learning supports and resources.

Identify Competencies: Identify individual, group, and organizational competencies that will improve recruitment, retention, well being, and performance.

Design and Implement Training Programs: Plan and deliver training, enabling co-workers to contribute to improved recruitment, retention, well being, and performance.

Figure 2.4   A Design Team Tool: Responsibilities of Each Design Team Member.

PAR mechanism. For example, a team may be able to work on important, concrete priorities such as improving job descriptions, improving working relationships, and defining responsibilities.

Mirroring the "baby steps" that mark progress with a "difficult" client, every small, team problem-solving success needs to be acknowledged and celebrated because each progressively helps propel the team to a new level of development and performance. In short, the social side of team development is integrated with the task side of team performance, and success breeds success. In other words, one-at-a-time "small wins" (Weick, 1984) foster team cohesion, enabling problem-solving progress and paving the way for future performance, while generating new knowledge as members learn. This is PAR in action.

DESIGN TEAM PARTICIPATORY ACTION RESEARCH
FACILITATION: PERSONAL REFLECTIONS

A closer look at team, facilitation is in order so that readers can better understand this special practice. team facilitation mirrors some of the needs and requirements in all manner of PAR initiatives. The following autobiographical narrative, based on the multiple experiences of Caringi (the second author of this chapter) with teams in New York and Montana, was developed with these two perspectives in mind.

I have helped teams collect and evaluate their baseline information (data) about retention and turnover. There is no one way to do this. The important thing is to do it in ways that enable teams to stay focused on their data. Without this unrelenting focus, they will resort to "he said, she said" rumors and personal impressions. When this situation develops, the research component of the team is lost.

In one county system, for example, I helped the team look at the survey research data provided by a university team. Team members added what was missing, and then they identified retention priorities. Examples of these priorities included workers' safety in the field, workers' salary, workers' stress, and job descriptions. With my help as a team facilitator, they focused on the "actionability" of each priority, that is, ones that were malleable and also ones that they could do something about.

For example, one team, determined that workers' salary was the most important retention/turnover priority. Before too long, team members tabled this salary priority because they did not view it as an "actionable" item. After all, salary increases would require action by the commissioner, and most important, the county legislature. In short, working on salary would take enormous time and would not yield immediate returns and benefits because so much influence and control resided outside the team and even the commissioner. So, this particular team, decided to keep salary on its "radar screen," but not to make it the first actionable priority. They placed it in a team planning parking lot. Subsequently, the team decided that "clear, coherent job descriptions" was the most actionable and important item they should work on.

All the while, I, the facilitator, was active in teaching the team why this was a good approach. During the second session, I introduced the concept of a logic model (W.K. Kellogg Foundation, 2004). I decided to introduce it at this second meeting because I determined that this team was ready for it, and also because we had enough time left to examine the concept. This logic model is an essential element of the design team process. Using intervention language, the logic model enables teams to understand the "theory of the problem" before designing and implementing solutions (i.e., interventions). I learned that facilitators can help team members understand this complex idea (theory of the problem) by asking three questions:

- What's wrong that needs fixing, and what are the causes?
- What's good and strong that needs to be kept as part of the solution?
- How can we be sure that the solution(s) we identify will fix the problem (i.e., to what extent does the solution address the causes)?

This logical, systematic approach is new to team members. It takes time, patience, and persistence to cultivate it. One reason that it takes time is that staff members in child welfare have seen many interventions come and go without real change. Many such change efforts were not well thought out from the beginning.

When I do this work with the logic model and emphasize its use in the team planning process, I am a teacher, a group process clinician, and a capacity-builder. By helping teams understand, endorse, and use the logic model template, I am, in essence, "teaching them to fish." In other words, I am preparing them to do more of this work on their own in the future (and after I leave). All in all, I aim to empower them for future, independent functioning and effective action—and with the aim of having the team become a sustainable fixture in the organization.

Initially, I explain all parts of the model to team members and entertain their questions. Because this process is new, we proceed slowly. There are many questions. It helps when we review a sample logic model developed by another team. Figure 2.5 provides an example. This model was "sanitized" for confidentiality, but it serves its purpose. It shows team members how others have proceeded, and, most important, it shows them that others have actually completed this difficult work.

Finally, I complete a team debriefing process so that members know that we have accomplished something important. I also prep the team for the next meeting. We set the agenda based on our need to work on their first logic model and to learn more about how to do this work efficiently, effectively, and successfully. Easy to write about, this this facilitation is enormously challenging. The facilitator learns and acquires expertise while practicing with the team.

I brought to team facilitation extensive experience with group practice. In comparison to my group practice, this design team facilitation is the most complex team and group leadership I have ever done. The mix of clinical and task orientations in an emotionally charged team development environment requires the facilitator to be absolutely on top of the game. To this end, facilitators need help, especially so at the beginning. For example, it is essential to have a colleague assist with note-taking. Notes serve as minutes and also primary data for the team. The work of facilitation requires that the primary facilitator be free of this work and able to concentrate on team formation and performance.

Significantly, team facilitators must be aware of their own emotional needs because this team facilitation involves an enormous amount of emotional labor. Trying to make a functioning team out of individuals who oftentimes do not get along can be an intense process because team members displace their anger and frustration. In fact, my coauthor and I have been yelled at numerous times in team meetings and even made to feel like we were one cause of the team's problems.

In order to not take this personally, facilitators must be prepared for surprising and unpleasant reactions from team members. Emotional labor, secondary trauma, lateral violence, and burnout are all frequent in team work (Caringi et al., 2012), and they affect facilitators as well as team members. The upshot is critically important: *DT facilitators must be knowledgeable about self-care for both themselves and the team.*

Need / problem	Causes	Effects on Retention	Ideal Situation	Solutions in place at one time or another	New Solutions Needed
1. There is a focus on negative feedback rather than positive strengths 2. There is a feeling that what we are doing or the way in which we are doing it is not "good enough"	1. Society as a whole, and Agency x DSS more specifically are focused on the negative. 2. We have learned how to asses the negative, but learning a new way of thinking and judging performance is a difficult task to accomplish	1. Workers feel devalued and inadequate 2. There is low morale in the agency which leads to job dissatisfaction and eventually turnover	1. There would be "warm fuzzies" given as positive feedback 2. There are naturally positive interactions that occur between supervisors and workers. 3. Supervisors provide workers with daily positive feedback that is visible. 4. Positive work environment where people are smiling, there is good team work, supportive coworkers and mutual acknowledgement of workloads.	1. There used to be a news letter "Treading Water" that would detail caseworker accomplishments, unit accomplishments, caseworker anniversaries, and birthdays. 2. Acknowledgement of work anniversaries 3. Once a month there is a coffee and donuts meeting where commissioner comes to speak with and encourage caseworkers	1. A positive feedback box outside of each unit supervisor's office where workers from that unit can write tell sup about positive things coworkers have done. (Secretaries can type up in a newsletter and hand out monthly) 2. Supervisors give stickers for positive accomplishments. The worker with the most stickers at the end of the month wins a much needed office supply ie (corkboard, stapler, white out pen, etc). It is delivered at the monthly staff meeting or can be posted in an email sent to everyone (including commissioner) each month 3. When a worker has gone above the call of duty, such as putting in extra hours a letter of recognition is placed in the employees file, with a copy to the employee and the commissioner.

5. There is acknowledgement from coworkers and supervisors	4. There are great emotional supports from coworkers 5. We have flex time which makes us feel appreciated 6. There have been certificates of appreciation given out to units in the past 7. Letters of recognition have gone in files in the past.	4. There is a monthly coffee and donut Friday where the first 20 minutes of the day is spent increasing unit morale. Caseworkers/units take turns bringing in food. 5. New and goods start off unit meetings. Each case worker says something new or good about their life for that day. 6. Employee of the quarter. Every three months one worker is nominated by their coworkers as the employee of the quarter for managing a tough case or being extra helpful. This person receives a $20 gift certificate to a local restaurant and is acknowledged at an end of the year caseworker reception thrown by the Agency 7. Have a rotating sticker fairy who puts stickies containing "warm fuzzies" on other's computers. 8. Supervisors put little sticky notes on work saying good court report/UCR, etc 9. Personally model positive feedback Have an occasional luncheon or reception for the entire staff to show appreciation and give positive feedback	

Figure 2.5 An Example of a Team-generated Logic Model.

EXAMPLES OF DESIGN TEAM IMPROVEMENTS AND INNOVATIONS

The external regulatory environment for public child welfare is an ever-present constraint. The civil service system and the Child and Family Services Reviews are special constraints. Add to these two constraints relevant state policy mandates, and the result is a limited number of options for dramatic team-generated innovations.

At the same time, facilitation for team formation and performance is like a developmental journey, one that mirrors three important aspects of clinical and direct practice with individual clients. Aspect 1: Start where the client is. Aspect 2: Start small on a manageable scale, where there is a high probability of success, and future opportunities will develop from today's small wins (Weick, 1984). Aspect 3: Focus on an actionable priority, that is, work on problems teams are able to solve.

All three aspects were instrumental in the examples of team-generated improvements and innovations outlined below. All derived from logic-model-guided action planning focused on what it will take to improve desirable workforce retention—and with the assumption that better outcomes for children and families hinge on a stable, high-quality workforce in a high-performing learning organization.

- One team developed a worker safety plan with particular reference to CPS investigations.
- Another team requested, planned, and helped to implement training for workers' secondary traumatic stress.
- Another team developed a new policy manual to cover all relevant workforce policies, together with a system to ensure that it remained updated.
- Yet another team focused on supervision, especially supervisory competence (in relation to recommended practice strategies); supervisory social support; and consistent, stable supervision so that front-line workers were able to learn and improve and a practice of front-liners' "shopping for their preferred supervisor" would end.
- Another team focused on consistency, clarity, and accuracy of communications from middle managers—once it was recognized that their biased preferences, not those of top-level leaders, were driving agency policy and practice.

- A rural team recommended changes in the parking places assigned to CPS workers. A minor change to an outsider, this was a major change to workers who needed to bring children to the agency and had to walk long distances with them in very bad weather.

- Another rural team recommended two major shifts, and both involved new relationships with the top-level leader (the commissioner). This team recommended and received approval for revised job descriptions and new decision-making protocols based on data.

All of these examples derived from team members' perceptions of their respective realities. In other words, the facilitator started where the team-as-client was, aiming for small wins and ensuring that every recommendation was actionable.

In this fashion, team facilitators improved communication and overall relationships among front-line workers, supervisors, and top-level leaders at the same time that genuine improvements were implemented. Each new improvement built team efficacy and contributed to workers' job satisfaction and sense of empowerment. The evidence indicates that desirable retention increased, at least in the short term, in particular agencies. The sobering reminder here is that high-turnover agencies known as workforce revolving doors present formidable challenges, and there are no easy answers, even with skillfully facilitated design teams. This finding is one contribution to knowledge development, and it sets the stage for future research and development.

EMERGENT CONTRIBUTIONS TO THEORY, RESEARCH, AND COMPREHENSIVE SYSTEMS CHANGE

PAR enables both knowledge generation and theory articulation as real-world problems are addressed. The PAR design teams described in this chapter were structured and evaluated accordingly. Due to space constraints, readers are referred to published evaluation studies, including the workforce advantages (e.g., improved job satisfaction and reduced turnover) and organizational benefits these studies have documented (Caringi et al., 2008; Claiborne et al., in press; Lawson et al., 2006; Strolin-Glotzman et al., 2009). Examples of these PAR teams' contributions to knowledge development and theory articulation provide a fitting conclusion to this chapter. Important in their own right, these examples can be viewed as progress markers and lessons learned in a design team PAR journey toward better problem solving, knowledge generation, and improved outcomes.

From a Technical Problem to an Adaptive One With Wicked Features

In the beginning, the twin challenge of improving desirable workforce retention and preventing undesirable turnover was framed as a technical problem. All relevant stakeholders—the researchers, agency heads, state agency department leaders—expected relatively straightforward solutions, that is, discrete retention/turnover interventions.

As the PAR teams continued with their work, and as the researchers gained new knowledge and understanding about participating agencies' respective workforce configurations and organizational designs, it became apparent that our original assumptions were not only unwarranted but also fundamentally flawed. The retention/turnover problem turned out to be nested in others, so much so that it had to be refined and freshly conceptualized in two ways.

The first conceptualization was emphasized in chapter 1. The retention/turnover priority was in some agencies an adaptive problem without easy answers. In other agencies, especially the ones with so much turnover that the researchers sometimes referred to them as "revolving door workforces," intractable high turnover turned out to be a wicked problem. Although PAR design teams made progress and generated new knowledge, they did not solve the turnover problem.

The second conceptualization derived readily from the first one. The retention/turnover problem in turnover-riddled and highly unstable agencies needed to be framed as a systems problem. Systems problems are multicomponent entities. Changes in one part of the system entail or necessitate changes in the others. In the same vein, attempts to change one part often are impeded and blocked by the actions of other parts (Foster-Fishman & Behrens, 2007).

Such was the contribution of the PAR design teams and companion research and development interventions undertaken with top-level leaders and front-line practice supervisors (Claiborne & Lawson, 2011. The examples provided below, important in their own right, should be viewed as components of a systems change agenda.

A Conceptual Map for Workforce Quality and Stability

Public sector bureaucracies in general and child welfare systems in particular tend to be riveted on a singular outcome domain. Outcomes for client systems, in this case children, youth, and families, are of paramount importance. In this conceptual framework, workforce outcomes are secondary—if they are emphasized at all.

Owing to the PAR design teams, the flaws in this dominant approach became apparent. To return to a main claim at the beginning of this chapter, workforce characteristics and outcomes need to be prioritized alongside child and family outcomes. Put differently, the two sets of outcomes are fundamentally interdependent; achieving one set depends on progress toward achieving the other one (Lawson et al., 2005).

A MULTIFACETED WORKFORCE DEVELOPMENT AND RECONFIGURATION AGENDA

Consistent with the above-referenced conceptual framework, and in contrast to the view of workforce retention/turnover as a narrow technical problem, the PAR design teams yielded both definitive knowledge and suggestive implications about the need for a more expansive and comprehensive agenda. Here, too, systems thinking and frameworks were needed because there were many parts, and the parts were connected.

The researchers settled on the following descriptors: workforce optimization, professionalization, and stabilization. Drawing on an interdisciplinary literature, while retaining a focus on the empirical data provided by the PAR design teams, the researchers derived an eight-component conceptual and operational framework for this workforce agenda (Lawson et al., 2005).

1. *Recruitment mechanisms:* What the agency does to attract suitable candidates;
2. *Selection mechanisms:* How the agency picks the best candidates from its pool—including the influence of civil service rules;
3. *Preparation mechanisms:* State and agency training and other preparation initiatives, especially university social work programs;
4. *Deployment mechanisms:* The extent to which both new and veteran workers are placed in the best jobs—ones that match their competencies and aspirations and also enable work-life balance—and also are not moved to other roles without their consent;
5. *Support mechanisms:* Starting with the agency's mechanisms for inducting and socializing new workers, these mechanisms span organizational structures and processes that provide supports, services, and resources to the workforce—and with a special priority for emotional labor supports and secondary traumatic stress prevention and alleviation;
6. *Advancement and enrichment mechanisms:* Mechanisms for supporting promotions, providing professional development, and capitalizing on workers' talents and aspirations to improve the agency;
7. *Succession-planning mechanisms:* Mechanisms for stabilizing the workforce in anticipation of retirements, resignations, and leaves; and
8. *Job redesign, workforce remodeling, and systems change mechanisms:* Mechanisms for improving jobs and changing the system of rules, roles, and relationships so that a more ideal system is progressively developed, especially one directed toward helping people in lieu of self-serving, people-processing routines.

These eight priorities are related, and they are not the final word on the subject. Future research and development initiatives may benefit from this framework at the same time that researchers pose alternatives and strive to provide additional details.

Vicious Cycles Caused by High, Undesirable Turnover

Researchers and agency leaders sometimes use the terms *ripple effect* or *spillover effect* when one problem is implicated in a causal chain.

Persistently high turnover is one such problem. The several PAR design teams examined in this study provide compelling examples of the ripple and spillover effects, albeit without a conceptual framework that mapped the pattern. University researchers are prepared to do this work, and the quality of their contributions is enhanced when the patterns are grounded in empirical findings.

Figure 2.6 depicts the vicious cycles that develop and gain traction in high-turnover child welfare agencies (Lawson et al., 2005). The several problem components in this figure are noteworthy, of course, but the overall pattern is the most significant element. This pattern implicates multiple aspects of the workforce, at all levels of the agency, as well as salient features of the agency as a work organization. In this conceptualization, a high level of undesirable workforce turnover is a wicked systems problem, one that requires multicomponent, complex interventions. Future research and development initiatives can be framed and designed accordingly.

An Early Warning and Rapid Response System for Retention Planning

The PAR design teams in the various agencies consistently provided an important insight with two sides. Oftentimes, co-workers knew of their colleagues' intention to leave long before they departed, and something could have been done to retain them if a system had been in place with caring, competent people who could make it work. Where desirable retention is concerned, intent to leave is a good predictor of actual turnover. One key to retention, it follows, is to develop an early warning and rapid response system (Lawson et al., 2005). Ideally, such a system would involve practical, valid language and include formal strategies for gathering retention and turnover data so that people could gain new knowledge and competence as their organizations strive to continually improve.

The PAR design teams examined provide important findings on these pertinent issues. Metaphorically, these findings are like pieces in search of a coherent puzzle. As with all manner of PAR investigations, the university-based researchers had to assume lead responsibility for the development of a conceptual framework—that is, the picture on the top of the puzzle box. These same researchers had to develop the parameters for an early warning and rapid response system for preventable, undesirable workforce turnover.

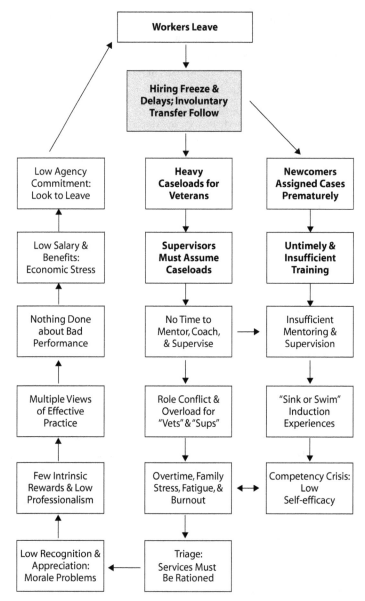

Figure 2.6 Staffing Problems as One Cause of Turnover's Vicious Cycles.

The researchers settled on a three-component framework (Lawson et al., 2005). First, *Push factors* are the organizational and environmental factors that cause people to look to leave or actually leave. Workers feel forced out because of problematic managerial styles, negative and defensive organizational cultures and climates, inadequate supervision, insufficient training, and lack of community supports and resources.

Second: *Pull factors* are the external environmental mechanisms that lure workers away, despite efforts to retain them. Pull factors include other jobs in the area, especially those in the human services that provide better working conditions, supports, and rewards. Other child welfare agencies also operate as pull factors. For example, rural PAR design teams indicated that some workers were lured away by an adjacent county agency. This is a different kind of turnover, and it needs to be understood because the overall pool of child welfare workers is not reduced when these moves occur.

Third: *Keep factors* are the mechanisms that enable commissioners, managers, and supervisors to become proactive in their efforts to retain staff. For example, work-life fit is a key reason why workers stay. Other keep factors are circumstantial and environmental. For example, lack of other jobs in the immediate vicinity, especially for people with firm local roots, is a keep factor.

Figure 2.7 provides team-generated examples of these three kinds of factors. Based on this significant contribution from teams in several

---

PUSH FACTORS: FEATURES OF THE AGENCY, JOB, WORK AND COMMUNITY THAT LEAD TO TURNOVER

- Inadequate salaries and benefits
- Heavy caseloads
- Heavy workloads caused in part by excessive, redundant paperwork
- Lack of safety protocols and supports at the office and in the field
- Stress, emotional exhaustion, and vicarious trauma induced by the work
- Lack of supports and interventions aimed at preventing burnout and trauma
- Lack of supportive and competent supervision
- Lack of support from co-workers
- "Tighten the screws", compliance-oriented supervision and management
- Lack of fit between career goals and actual job and work requirements
- Perceptions of unjust practices (e.g., assigning caseloads, granting promotions)

Figure 2.7 Toward an Early Warning and Rapid Response System in Retention Planning.

- An agency-wide emphasis on people processing instead of people changing practice
- For workers with MSW's, lack of opportunities to use their knowledge and skills
- Lack of solid, effective working relationships with other systems (e.g., courts, schools)

PULL FACTORS: EXTERNAL FEATURES AND FORCES THAT LURE PEOPLE AWAY

- A better job offer from another child welfare agency in the community
- A better job offer a different community agency
- The lure of moving to a different community where one's family is located
- The lure of higher salary and more vacation time provided by a local business
- The lure of private social work practice with mental health clients

KEEP FACTORS: INTERNAL AND EXTERNAL FORCES AND FACTORS THAT ENCOURAGE RETENTION

1. *Factors the agency can influence and control: Hence, retention planning priorities*
   - Effective improvements focused on the retention priorities in Figures 5-9 in this report
   - Public child welfare is a career, not just a job, because the agency supports and promotes career development
   - Adequate wages and benefits
   - Mechanisms for recruitment, selection, state and local training, organizational socialization, and job placements are aligned and harmonized.
   - Caseworkers, supervisors and managers perceive that the agency supports them
   - Workers are provided with suitable office space and equipment and good transportation
   - A "can do" attitude—individual and collective efficacy—is pervasive in the agency

   - Supervision is both supportive and competent, and supervisors' loads are manageable
   - Caseloads are harmonized with overall workloads, and both are manageable
   - Life-work fit is an organizational priority, and workers have "say so" in improving it
   - Workers at all levels of the agency are rewarded for competent practice and recognized for their extraordinary achievements
   - Burnout, stress, and trauma prevention and reduction interventions are readily available
   - The agency provides safety protections in the office and in the field
   - The agency and its workers enjoy solid, effective ties with other service systems, enabling case coordination and collaboration to meet clients' co-occurring needs
   - The agency's climate and culture are nurturing, positive, and proactive
2. *Factors outside the agency's influence and control*
   - Lack of other job opportunities in the area
   - Firm ties to the community through two-career relationships and family needs

Figure 2.7 (Continued)

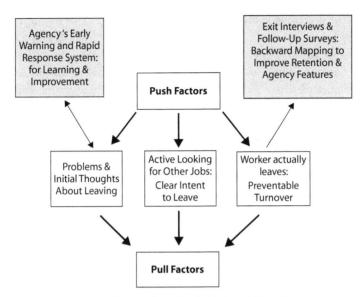

Figure 2.8 Team-generated Examples of Push, Pull, and Keep Factors.

agencies, the university researchers were able to develop an operational framework for a retention/turnover early detection and rapid response system. Figure 2.8 provides an overview.

The preceding examples are merely representative. Readers interested in this line of research are encouraged to visit the references provided throughout this chapter for more examples and salient details. Together, these examples of actionable knowledge and theory attest to the power of PAR design teams as well as their import for all manner of public sector bureaucracies, especially child welfare.

CONCLUDING OBSERVATIONS

PAR design teams are not panaceas for the challenges manifest in public child welfare, but their importance should not be discounted. This chapter has provided examples of how and why teams offer manifold contributions to knowledge generation, theory articulation, organizational and workforce intervention development, and policy change. Ultimately, both workers in the system and the vulnerable children, youth, and families will benefit from effective PAR design teams.

The preceding analysis, like those in the chapters that follow, does not address an important issue. Should PAR participants be listed as coauthors of all relevant scholarly presentations and publications? There are no easy answers to this question. In our work with design teams we sometimes have shared authorship for scholarly and professional presentations. In fact, we have provided travel support to professional meetings for representative team members and their agency leaders. However, we have not yet shared authorship for scholarly publications, especially those that articulate scientific theory. In our view, university researchers are uniquely prepared for this PAR-driven theory development, which requires a complex combination of inductive and deductive reasoning, together with a significant grounding in the related research literature. Of course, ours is not the only view, and it is not automatically the correct or best one. Readers need to know about the issue and contemplate their own views and research strategy.

Clearly, PAR design teams have considerable potential for the work that lies ahead in all public sector agencies, including schools, juvenile justice organizations, domestic violence agencies, and substance abuse treatment centers When such a broad view is entertained, the examples provided herewith do not represent teams' full potential. One reason is that the researchers and team facilitators doing the work described in this chapter were genuinely pioneers. More concretely, the initial team facilitators did not have ready access to the several available tools and conceptual frameworks presented in this chapter and in other publications (Lawson & Caringi, 2008). These initial facilitators had to design tools and test ideas so that others, including you, the reader, could benefit from them. Such is the nature of science. It is a collective endeavor with cumulative achievements over time—and with succeeding initiatives benefiting from their predecessors (Kuhn, 1996).

Another reason for this untapped potential is especially important. The PAR design teams described in this chapter were constrained in three important ways. To begin with, they often focused on problems permitted and identified by top-level agency leaders.

Moreover, teams were restricted to the priorities that team members and facilitators viewed to be "malleable" and "actionable." Put differently, teams focused on a restricted number of priorities, ones that team members and facilitators perceived that they could do something about.

In an ideal world, all problems, needs, and opportunities are open to team problem-solving and knowledge generation. Finally, PAR design teams were time-limited social experiments. This temporary status contrasts with the ideals of the industrial democracy movement envisioned by Lewin, Emery, and Trist. In these pioneering leaders' views, PAR teams were permanent fixtures in democratic work organizations, both public and private. To reiterate, PAR teams promised to democratize the workplace because they provided workers with genuine voice and choice, real decision-making power and authority.

Arguably, in today's era of social networks facilitated by information age technologies, PAR design teams' research and development potential can be realized in new and exciting ways. After all, these networks develop and operate both inside and outside organizations, oftentimes connecting people in distant places around shared needs, concerns, and aspirations. Exciting possibilities accompany the development of networked design teams that are not restricted to a particular place and a single organization. If this chapter contributes to this all-important agenda by helping readers gain a compelling vision and develop the requisite commitments and preliminary competence for team formation, development, and optimization, it has achieved its primary aim. If it also results in PAR-generated improvements in child welfare systems, benefiting vulnerable people and child welfare professionals alike, so much the better.

3

Participatory Action Research with Youth

Christine T. Bozlak and Michele A. Kelley

INTRODUCTION

A review of the growing body of research on adolescents yields three important findings. First, studies have been conducted "on" adolescents. That is, in the vast majority of studies, young people have been viewed and treated as "subjects" and "research participants."

Second, studies have focused on the analysis of young people's problems, and with particular interest in how problems, individually and together, have affected this population's well-being. So, for example, researchers have explored problems such as substance use, risky sexual behaviors, and mental health concerns. Overall, this line of research has resulted in an abundance of studies that detail the prevalence of problems, including social analyses of their antecedents, correlates, causes, and outcomes. However, these studies have not been participatory, participant driven, and action oriented. Consequently, their contributions to solutions have been limited to problem framing and analysis.

The third finding is that these problem-focused studies have outnumbered those focused on questions regarding how to adequately prepare and equip individuals, especially adolescents, to thrive in life. In other words, one could say that there has been too much focus on adolescent-related problems in the present at the expense of studies focused on building youth's capacity to make a positive difference in the here and now, while also building their skills for a successful and healthy adulthood.

These three findings frame and illuminate this chapter's approach to participatory action research (PAR). Henceforth, this approach will be called youth participatory action research, using the acronym YPAR (Cammarota & Fine, 2008). YPAR, it shall become apparent, enfranchises youth as co-researchers. It also builds on their strengths in lieu of emphasizing their problems. Significantly, YPAR is structured to yield solutions (interventions) to significant problems that affect young people's well-being, while at the same time providing them with the knowledge, skills, and abilities they need to thrive in life.

Other PAR experts have written noteworthy contributions on YPAR, and readers should review their work (e.g., Cammarota & Fine, 2008; Ginwright, Noguera, & Cammarota, 2006; Leadbeater et al., 2006). The progression for our chapter is as follows: We begin by describing the importance of utilizing a PAR approach with youth, and we provide examples of YPAR studies. Then, we provide two examples of YPAR, both of which we conducted in community settings. We conclude with lessons we learned in conducting YPAR. We also offer recommendations for making adolescent research increasingly translational and action oriented, and most important, recommendations for new YPAR designs that are more empowering for adolescent participants.

Our primary orientation throughout can be viewed as a public health approach. This forthright acknowledgment is not a serious limitation, because the boundaries between public health and social work increasingly are being bridged, especially so when the vulnerable people residing in challenging places are of interest and empowerment-oriented interventions and helping strategies are prioritized. It also is noteworthy that the second author is both a clinical and public health social worker who brings a social work perspective to YPAR.

In the same vein, when YPAR is conducted with vulnerable youth living in challenging places, the salience of any one discipline diminishes.

After all, youth are vulnerable in part because challenging places give rise to multiple, co-occurring needs that transcend the boundaries of any one discipline. Interdisciplinary YPAR is a practical necessity.

We also indicate how and why local assets, such as community-based organizations, can mediate social disadvantage and marginalization and serve as effective partners for YPAR. Where asset- and strengths-based research and practice are concerned, social work is at the forefront. The work of the Social Development Research Group at the University of Washington stands as one prominent example (Catalano, Berglund, Ryan, Lonczak, & Hawkins, 2004; Checkoway & Gutierrez, 2006), and another is provided by the Association for Community Organization and Social Administration's *Journal of Community Practice*. Ultimately, YPAR can be framed as interdisciplinary and anti-oppressive work (Sakamoto & Pitner, 2005). It involves and requires social work, but it also transcends it.

INTERRUPTING AN ESTABLISHED RESEARCH TRADITION: THE IMPORTANCE OF CONDUCTING YPAR

There has been an identifiable tendency in the research traditions of various helping disciplines dedicated to improving the human condition. The tendency has been to focus exclusively on alleviating population-based problems, oftentimes including deficit-based assumptions about these populations. Especially in clinical research, researchers have focused on understanding a problem or deficit as a medical condition. Proceeding with a disease metaphor, these researchers have investigated how to treat it (Rotegard, Moore, Fagermoen, & Ruland, 2010).

Social work research has followed a different trajectory. Although there has been an increased emphasis on advocacy resulting from research, researchers have focused on understanding a social problem. (Intervention researchers obviously are an exception to this pattern.) For example, researchers have focused on poverty, aiming to identify and explain the reasons for people's low incomes (Maschi & Youdin, 2012). And in adolescent research, researchers predominantly have focused on the problems experienced within this population. They have emphasized the "risk behaviors" responsible for these problems, and sometimes the developmental causes of these behaviors. In sum, researchers often have taken a deficit approach to understanding people within their social settings and circumstances (Morgan & Ziglio, 2007)—known as a human behavior in the social environment perspective. In brief, researchers now acknowledge that the research with this population has often been conducted under the premise that adolescents are "social problems" (Raby, 2007, p. 48). This approach has led to adolescents being controlled with limited opportunities to represent their own interests in the research process (Raby, 2007).

Although psychiatry has been credited with initiating the concept of *assets*, or *health assets,* in the middle of the twentieth century (Rotegard et al., 2010), many disciplines have since prioritized this important concept. Assets refer to "the collective resources which individuals and communities have at their disposal, which protect against negative health outcomes and promote health status" (Glasgow Centre for Population Health, 2011, p. 2). This focus on health assets has ushered in two new priorities. One is to prevent negative health outcomes and adverse social circumstances, and the other is to empower individuals to reach their full potential to be contributing members of society.

The 1986 Ottawa Charter for Health Promotion (World Health Organization, 2014) often is credited as one of the driving forces of this asset-based and empowerment approach to health. For example, this asset-based approach to human research now serves as the impetus for clinical studies on patient empowerment for the prevention and management of illness (Rotegard et al., 2010); for social work studies focused on the advancement of human rights and social justice (Maschi & Youdin, 2012); and for both discipline-specific and interdisciplinary adolescent research that involves youth in the design and implementation of the research to investigate how youth assets can be mobilized for the prevention of the recurrent negative outcomes for this population and their communities (Amsden & VanWynsberghe, 2005). The implication is that if assets such as school and family connectedness among youth are fully realized, then these same assets will serve as "protective factors" (DiClemente, Santelli, & Crosby, 2009) for certain negative health behaviors and outcomes, thereby negating the need to confront the problem.

This asset-based approach to practice and research has coincided with the growing positive youth development (PYD) movement. PYD is defined in various ways. However, the working definition for the purpose of this chapter is "a philosophy or approach promoting a set of guidelines on how a community can support its young people so that they can grow up competent and healthy and develop to their full potential" (ACT for Youth resource manual, n.d.). A primary PYD principle is the empowerment of youth in all their environmental settings and developmental contexts. This genus of PYD has become a social movement involving governmental and non-governmental entities throughout the nation and the world. These entities include the National Association of County and City Health Officials (NACCHO) with its policy statement *Positive Youth Development Approaches in Adolescent Health Programs* (available at: http://www.naccho.org/advocacy/positions/upload/09-0 5-Positive-Youth-Development.pdf).

Just two nations in the world community have failed to ratify this agenda: the United States and Somalia. Even so, worldwide support for the active engagement of children and youth in their own livelihood and issues related to their well-being are well accepted, and they are institutionalized through the United Nations Convention on the Rights of the Child. YPAR has the potential to be a concrete mechanism to operationalize all such ideals.

YPAR AS POTENTIAL EMPOWERMENT OF YOUTH

In chapter 2, the two important regulative rules for PAR were emphasized. One is "ensuring that all participants enjoy voice and choice" (p. 11) regarding every aspect of the research investigation, and the other is sharing power and control whenever possible. Both rules apply when YPAR is designed and conducted, and for good reason. Traditional research has failed to engage youth as co-investigators in the research process; it has been conducted *on* (rather than *with*) youth, excluding their subjective experiences and perceptions (Best, 2007). Regarding this last point, typically, when a child or adolescent's perspective has been of interest, researchers have used a surrogate respondent. Surrogate respondents often have been a caregiver (typically a parent) or other authority figure in the individual's life, such as a teacher or coach. This is problematic because it makes the data less valid, and it further separates the youth from the research project.

PAR is a preferred research method for those researchers wishing to treat youth as participants in the research process, rather than human subjects to study (Raby, 2007). It also is the method of choice when youth's voices need to be heard, as opposed to the adult-as-youth voice.

YPAR aims to engage youth in as many aspects of the research process as possible. Ideally, this active engagement—not token involvement—includes the formation of the research question, the design and implementation of the study, the analysis and dissemination of the findings, and the action resulting from the study. Involving youth in this iterative manner allows for a developmental trajectory whereby youth gain more voice, choice, and power with each iteration.

The goals for each YPAR initiative vary. They are aligned in that they all aim to advance the PYD movement by contributing to knowledge on youth, while at the same time enabling them to gain skills in science, critical inquiry, and social justice, among other areas (Cammarota & Fine, 2008).

Easy to write about, YPAR is not easy to develop and implement. Despite the best efforts of well-intentioned researchers, formidable challenges are unavoidable, and so are several institutional barriers associated with university research infrastructures and regulations. For example, many entities related to the research process, including institutional review boards (IRBs), funders, and administrators, are not familiar with the PYD movement. The concept that youth need to be allowed to be active participants and co-investigators in research related to their well-being is nothing short of revolutionary.

This lack of familiarity with the PYD movement is coupled with university regulations for "conducting research on minors" (as typically phrased in the IRB process) and the need for informed consent from parents or legal guardians. Although all such barriers present both real and perceived challenges to YPAR, these limitations are surmountable. (The last chapter of this book provides some examples.) The following section highlights some of the YPAR studies that have already been conducted on a variety of topics. They demonstrate its feasibility and contributions to the knowledge of adolescence as a key developmental time period.

EXAMPLES OF YPAR FROM THE LITERATURE

Emerging examples of YPAR projects from a variety of fields, including social work, public health, and education, signal its considerable potential. The literature on youth as active participants in community-based change initiatives, including YPAR approaches, is replete with exemplars from social work scholars and practitioners. For example, Delgado and Zhou (2008) authored a book on youth-led health promotion that provides extensive guidance for engaging youth as assets in community inquiry that can lead to improvements in local policy and environmental change toward community health improvement.

Also, Roderick Watts has published extensively on youth sociopolitical development (SPD) (Watts, Diemer, & Voigt, 2011; Watts & Flanagan, 2007). An important concept in youth engagement in change-oriented research such as YPAR, SPD can assist scholars and practitioners in understanding the processes by which youth identify with social justice activism and make positive changes within their communities.

Likewise, Barry Checkoway has elaborated on the concept of youth participation. He identifies the scientific and ethical arguments for inclusion of youth in civic matters and policy (whether research or practice) that affect them, their families, and their communities (Checkoway, 2011; Checkoway, Allison, & Montoya, 2005). Along with Lorraine Gutiérrez, Checkoway edited a special volume of the *Journal of Community Practice* entitled "Youth Participation and Community Change," which was also published as a book of the same name (Checkoway & Guitérrez, 2011). Of particular interest is the introductory chapter, which summarizes key concepts and content in the book, including youth as citizens, youth contributions to society (a premise of YPAR), developmental and empowerment paradigms, and methods for engaging youth in change-oriented research and practice.

In the same vein, public health researchers have utilized YPAR to achieve a variety of goals. These goals include identifying the needs of youth, designing interventions, and providing feedback (Foster-Fishman et al., 2010); developing youth violence prevention programs (Leff et al., 2010); and conducting a participatory needs assessment of young injecting drug users (Coupland et al., 2005). To keep pace with evolving technologies and to adapt PAR to the interests and behaviors of youth, "e-PAR" methodologies, such as the model advanced by Flicker et al. (2008), are also in development. The e-PAR model is described as "engaging young people using youth media to identify, understand and describe structural and proximal issues of concern in their community and then develop action strategies for change" (Flicker et al., 2008, p. 289).

Educational researchers have sometimes grounded YPAR in the critical pedagogy advanced by Paulo Freire (2003). YPAR initiatives structured in relation to a revolutionary approach to reforming the educational system and addressing social injustices are especially salient (Cammarota & Fine, 2008). For example, researchers have used YPAR with marginalized segments of the adolescent population, such as urban minority youth, to address racial inequities in the educational system (e.g., Checkoway & Richards-Schuster, 2006).

Overall, YPAR studies differ in terms of age of the youth participants, methodologies, and findings. Other differences derive from the disciplinary affiliations of the researchers (e.g., education, public health, social work). Notwithstanding differences, these studies are similar in that their goals are to empower the youth participants, lead to an action (often a solution to a need or problem), and create scientific knowledge. Moreover, nearly every YPAR researcher likely will emphasize the rewards of this kind of research even as they lament the institutional barriers they needed to address in order to do this important work.

Our work with YPAR follows suit. In the following two sections, we provide two examples of YPAR studies that we conducted in a community setting outside Chicago, Illinois. As will become evident, neither study reached an "ideal" level of youth participation. However, both studies enabled the first author, Bozlak, then a doctoral student under the guidance of the second author, Kelley (her doctoral advisor during the studies), to be challenged to achieve an increased level of youth participation in an asset-based study designed to improve the overall well-being of the youth and their residential community. We present these two case examples to illustrate YPAR concepts and to encourage the reader to consider possibilities for enabling YPAR in their communities of interest.

Case Example One: Youth Participation in a Clean Indoor
Air Ordinance Campaign

Basic Design and Purpose of Study

Exposure to environmental tobacco smoke (ETS, or secondhand smoke) is recognized worldwide as a significant threat to population health, and elimination of ETS is part of comprehensive tobacco control policies (U.S. Department of Health and Human Services, 2006; World Health Organization, 2014). Children and youth are particularly vulnerable to the harmful effects of tobacco, as well as the marketing of tobacco products (Centers for Disease Control and Prevention [CDC], 2010). Exposure to ETS has been steadily decreasing over the past decade due to tobacco control policies that prohibit smoking in workplaces, restaurants, and public spaces (U.S. Department of Health and Human Services).

A group of concerned local residents recruited a group of high school students in suburban Cook County, Illinois, to participate in a grassroots community-wide campaign to pass a clean indoor air ordinance. Their intent was to eliminate ETS in indoor public spaces, such as restaurants and other local worksites. To achieve this goal, the local governing body (Village Board of Trustees) needed to approve a clean indoor air ordinance. The new ordinance would ban ETS in designated indoor public spaces and at a specified distance from entrances. Throughout this campaign's duration, adults, including the first author, and youth were directly involved.

The involvement of youth in the campaign was important for three reasons. First, youth were natural allies and ambassadors in this local public health policy initiative (CDC, 2010). They were connected intergenerationally to their households and neighborhoods, and they could articulate the rationale for the campaign to their kin and neighbor networks. They could also engage these networks in action for change.

Second, youth participation is a values-based approach to any local effort to improve community health and well-being, as described in the previous section. In particular, youth are themselves vulnerable to ETS and have higher exposure rates than adults (CDC, 2010). Consequently, this public health issue was salient to youth once adult campaign members educated them about their vulnerability to ETS exposure, and then augmented their ability to take action against it.

Third, youth involvement in local action to improve population health engages the youth in envisioning future possibilities for themselves. Such a practical exercise in civic engagement can be a useful demonstration of their capacity to make contributions to society (Ginwright, Noguera, & Cammarota, 2006). Such civic action is especially noteworthy in building their future education and career aspirations (Watts & Flanagan, 2007). The rationale just provided offers a meaningful context for the following case summary of this limited but powerful YPAR project.

The community campaign consisted of a coalition of adult residents. Some were public health professionals. Others were current students and recent graduates from the local high school. The grassroots campaign was a volunteer-based political action initiative. The political goal was to pass a clean indoor air ordinance to regulate ETS in indoor public places and at worksites, including the regulation of ETS within the entranceway to these places.

Although the membership in the campaign was variable over the course of three years (2003–2006), a stable, committed group of adults remained throughout the campaign. Youth were involved in the campaign for the last two years of its duration. Youth, under the oversight of a designated adult campaign member, were involved in various activities throughout the community to gain residents' support for the ordinance.

We took the opportunity of this organic local experience in community health improvement, of which youth were an integral part, to document lessons learned in order to build local capacity for future adult-youth collaborations. Our goal was also to contribute to the evolving public health science on youth participation. The first author served in a participant-observer role, because she was a member of the campaign and was the lead investigator for this study. The second author was the first author's doctoral advisor and coinvestigator on this study. We conducted a qualitative formative evaluation to document youth participation, contributions, and reflections regarding the ongoing campaign and to utilize the findings to inform future campaign actions. We also wanted to build on the evolving knowledge of youth as active change agents in community health initiatives.

The first author consulted with her fellow campaign members about the value of the study to the campaign prior to initiating it. Youth campaign members were recruited to participate in one of two small group discussions, and adult campaign members were recruited to participate in telephone or in-person interviews. Details of the study methods are found in Bozlak and Kelley (2010). Here, we report on lessons learned and argue for the inclusion of youth in local initiatives to improve community well-being, using concepts from YPAR.

Knowledge Gained and Action Taken

Three major themes were derived from the data collected through youth group discussions and interviews with the adult members of the campaign.

Youth Motivation for Involvement in the Campaign. The campaign organizers provided small financial incentives to enhance the youth's interest in participating in the campaign. However, these incentives were not the primary reason the youth stayed engaged. Many of them found the topic of tobacco to be personally salient due to the presence of lung disease in their primary reference groups (peers, family).

The idea of prosocial civic action also appealed to the youth. They witnessed one another's passion and at times struggles with the campaign, as they all had the common experience of recently witnessing a defeat of the proposed clean indoor air ordinance. This experience led to renewed commitment to the campaign. The youth recognized that they were part of a group that included committed adults who valued youth participation. They saw an opportunity to contribute to their community through the campaign and its success.

Engaging and Maintaining Youth Involvement. Youth social networks were key to reinforcing the positive experiences of belonging and sense of purpose in the coalition's work. The youth's peers were supportive, and it appeared that many participants knew each other prior to participation in the coalition. In several cases, youth recruited other youth, particularly their friends, to participate in the campaign. In other cases, adult campaign members recruited youth they knew or even their own children.

Youth Contributions to the Campaign. The youth recognized their contributions to the campaign. Specifically, the tasks they completed (distributing flyers, canvassing the community, talking to community leaders about the importance of the issue, educating residents about the need for the ordinance) were instrumental in their development as active members of the community.

Adult members of the campaign also saw the broader impact of the youth's work. These adults recognized that it was the youth that gave credibility to the campaign, and that it was the youth who were, as one adult research participant put it, "the foot soldiers in the smoke-free army." It was also the framing of the issue as an adolescent and workplace health issue that contributed to the passage of the ordinance. For example, one of the Village Board of Trustees members publicly stated that he supported the ordinance because he recalled being an adolescent employed in a workplace that allowed smoking. Due to this employment, he experienced health-related issues. This experience led to concerns for himself and for others in workplaces that allowed smoking.

Barriers/Constraints to Conducting the Research as a YPAR Study

Because of time constraints, the group discussions with the youth were held at only one point in the campaign. Group discussions held throughout the campaign would have allowed for a better understanding of the youth engagement in the campaign. However, the timeliness of the discussions provided immediate feedback to the campaign to help reenergize the campaign after the initial attempt at the ordinance was defeated. The first author shared the initial findings from the study with adult and youth representatives of the campaign in a member-checking process (Harper & Cole, 2012). Member checking is a process in qualitative research whereby the research participants are allowed the opportunity to review the research results for accuracy (Harper & Cole, 2012). Ideally, it results in consensus validation. Had there been an opportunity to hold follow-up discussion groups at the conclusion of the successful campaign, it could have been possible to see an increase in critical consciousness and sociopolitical development, two parameters which undergird pro-social action and civic engagement in youth (Ginwright et al., 2006).

The youth did not have the opportunity to shape the discussion guide prior to the group discussion sessions. In YPAR projects, it is recommended that participants be actively engaged in research design. In this study, the IRB insisted on using a preapproved discussion guide, and time constraints did not allow for an iterative construction of a final guide by youth participants prior to submission for review. It was necessary to move to the field quickly for data collection after IRB approval in order for the findings to inform the next steps of the campaign. However, youth participants in this research had no difficulty reflecting on the discussion questions pertaining to the campaign and their participation. They also appeared comfortable participating in the group discussion with their peers who were also youth campaign members.

We recognize the limitations of our engagement with youth in this study. We did not participate in inviting youth to be members of the campaign. The founders of the campaign initiated the recruitment of youth through their existing relationships with them in the community and social networks. If we had been involved at the beginning of the campaign, we would have recommended a more structured approach to youth governance in the campaign. We might have also planned for this formative evaluation of youth participation prior to the campaign's initiation. Nonetheless, the youth involved provided valuable feedback and insight to keep youth engaged and to help the campaign move forward.

Although youth engagement in the research design process was limited, many of the youth participants' activities during the study and during the design of the study satisfied elements of the regulative rules of PAR (see chapter 1). Specifically, the research focused on youth participation in the campaign. Youth participated in group interviews to better understand their involvement in the campaign, and they assisted in the member checking of the study's findings. The youth also participated in a discussion to reflect upon the study's findings and determine the next steps for the campaign. The youth participants expressed enthusiasm and support for the study throughout its duration.

Moreover, the first author was an active member in the campaign and participated in campaign activities that included the youth. Most important, the findings from the study helped to rejuvenate the campaign after the initial defeat of the ordinance by demonstrating the commitment the youth, as well as the adults, had to the ordinance and to the community's well-being. The ordinance passed on its second introduction before the Village Board of Trustees. Thus, a significant action resulted from the complementary nature of the study with the existing campaign structure and commitment by its members.

In summary, this study was an opportunity to observe and capture an organic community action strategy involving youth. It was also an opportunity for us to familiarize ourselves with the concepts of youth participation and PAR. Lessons learned through a YPAR-influenced formative evaluation informed both community health science generally as well as the course of the campaign specifically because the findings demonstrated the continued commitment that the youth, and others, had to the campaign and to the issue—despite the initial failed attempt at passing the ordinance. In 2010, the CDC published a best practices document that detailed the importance of engaging youth in tobacco control, especially tobacco-related policy at all levels of government, and the benefits of this engagement for both the youth and the community (CDC, 2010). YPAR is one opportunity to engage youth in public health efforts aimed to control tobacco in our communities and protect the health of society's most vulnerable citizens.

Case Example Two—Early Adolescents' Representations of Wellness

Basic Design and Purpose of Study

This second example was designed by the first author for her dissertation research. This study was a PAR investigation using qualitative methods: Photovoice and Literacy Through Photography. Together, these two methods enabled the achievement of four research goals. These goals were to (a) demonstrate the socially constructed meanings, or social representations, a purposive sample of youth (ages 9–11) gave to the concept "wellness" in their everyday lives; (b) determine how their conceptualization of wellness changed over time using the methodologies; (c) capture their personal impressions and shared understandings of how their settings affect their wellness; and (d) obtain their recommendations for the enhancement of their settings in order to promote wellness.

The context is an important part of the study. The Child Nutrition Act of 2004 mandated the creation of wellness policies in all school districts to improve the health of students, and it encouraged youth participation in their creation. Initial reports indicated there was a lack of youth participation in community wellness discussions. In addition, wellness is narrowly conceptualized in school district wellness policies.

The goal of this YPAR project was to allow youth to participate in an ongoing community wellness dialogue, resulting in a better understanding of how a group of youth ages 9–11 socially construct "wellness" in order to move a community to further action toward overall wellness enhancement (Cowen, 2000; Herr & Anderson, 2005; Strack, Magill, & McDonagh, 2004). This study qualified as a YPAR study because the first author was an active member in a community wellness coalition led by the research setting, a local community-based organization, for several years before study implementation. Bozlak also understood the need for this study through her participation and previous residence within the community. She thus engaged in discussions with community members during all phases of this study and incorporated their input. In addition, a goal of this study was to share the findings with the community members in the research setting for further action (Herr & Anderson, 2005).

We designed this study to serve as a model, or case example, for other communities incorporating youth participation into their wellness policy discussions. A case study is often viewed as a research approach utilizing a variety of methodologies (Eisenhardt, 2002). It can be defined as "a specific way of collecting, organizing, and analyzing data; in that sense it represents an analysis process" (Patton, 2002, p. 447). In this study, the case was one group of ten youths, ages 9–11, in one after-school youth and family-serving organization in the community.

In terms of the methodology, photovoice is based on the Freirian concept of "education for critical consciousness" (Freire, 1974; Wang, 1999). As a PAR methodology, photovoice is designed to allow for reflection, dialogue, and community transformation (Wang, 1999), all of which are central tenets of Friere's problem-posing pedagogical approach to education (Freire, 2003). In brief, research participants are given cameras to photograph a specific research theme. Participants are also engaged in the analysis of the photographs using the SHOWeD method to reflect upon and analyze their images. Typically, a photography exhibit that allows for advocacy opportunities with decision-makers on the subject matter occurs at the end of the project.

Literacy Through Photography, as developed by renowned children's photographer Wendy Ewald, informed this study. Ewald views photography as "the most democratic visual art of our time" (Ewald, 2001, p. 14). Here, individuals of various ages and skill levels can take photographs of what is physically present and what one conceptualizes. Ewald recognized that photography can help children to become more literate because often seeing a visual image of something helps children to be

Table 3.1 Data Collection Session Descriptions

Data Collection Session	Description of Activity
1	Introduction; Writing Assignment, Photography Instruction
2	Discuss writing assignment; Photography group outing in community
3	Bus outing to take photographs in the community; sites selected by youth
4	Distribution of photos—SHOWeD analysis by youth
5	Peer exhibit; Group discussion
6	Adult community leader exhibit and discussion
7	Debriefing and Questionnaire completion; Distributed incentives

able to be more expressive in written narrative form, especially when the image pertains to something relevant to their own lives.

Over time, Ewald created Literacy Through Photography (LTP) and the Duke University LTP workshop (Ewald, 2001). Ewald's Literacy Through Photography approach to teaching photography to children "grew out of an attempt to address what [she] saw as the need to attend to our neglected physical and visual surroundings, and the need we all feel to articulate and communicate something relevant about our personal and communal lives" (Ewald, 2001, p.8).

The first author participated in a Literacy Through Photography workshop with Ewald prior to designing this study, and elements of the LTP process were incorporated into the study design. Table 3.1 describes the data collection sessions that took place as part of this study.

Knowledge Gained and Action Taken

The youth in this study conceptualized wellness in three dimensions: personal, relational, and collective (Prilleltensky & Fox, 2007). Their wellness themes can be categorized into the following areas: environment, physical activity, safety, food, freedom, self-directed learning opportunities, transportation, inner life/spirituality, and positive social relationships. The youth participants recommended a variety of changes to enhance their settings' ability to promote wellness.

For example, participants stressed the need for access to nature, especially green space for physical activity, and active transportation opportunities. They stated that recess, physical education, and healthy food options are important in the school setting. They also saw the value in community settings and resources that create opportunities for self-directed learning. Finally, the youth acknowledged that wellness is a social justice issue, because some of their peers live in areas that promote violence rather than safety and well-being.

The results from this study demonstrate that youth view wellness as more than just nutrition and physical activity, which typically are the primary components of most school wellness policies. One implication is that any comprehensive wellness policy should be developed utilizing a more holistic conceptualization of the term. The youth expressed that their settings can have an impact on wellness, a concept congruent with the social ecological approach in health promotion. This study's findings demonstrate that youth are able to conceptualize abstract concepts, articulate complex thoughts, and make a significant contribution to their community through engaging in discussions. Through this study, we also prepared the youth for critical decisions that influence their well-being and others'.

This study was presented three times to external audiences. The first of these was during data collection when the youth participants presented a photo exhibit to adult community leaders and then participated in a group discussion with them. The first author was also invited to a local school district meeting to present the results of the study. Finally, the research setting hosted a community meeting for the presentation of the study results. Youth research participants and their families were also invited to attend.

Barriers to Conducting the Research as a YPAR Study

Although many types of PAR exist, this second study is not a "pure" YPAR study (Herr & Anderson, 2005, p. 101) because the participant co-researchers were not consulted about the study design from its beginning. More specifically, they were not asked if the phenomenon of interest was something they prioritize. However, it appeared from their verbal reflections that this PAR project was of interest and of value to them because it gave them an opportunity they might not have had otherwise to participate in a wellness policy development process being imposed on them by the federal and state governments.

Other limitations of this study also are instructive for readers. The IRB approval process was lengthy and required a series of applications to the full, convened board, as well as through the expedited route. The final approved IRB application required the majority of the study to be planned prior to recruiting the youth participants. This detracted from the participatory nature of the study because the study design decisions had to be made by the research setting staff and the researchers, and not in collaboration with the youth.

The IRB also required the investigator to develop photography guidelines, and IRB members insisted on their approval prior to data collection. This administrative hurdle resulted in restrictions on what the youth could and could not photograph. In this way, the IRB fundamentally limited this YPAR study.

During the project debriefing, the youth remarked that the photography guidelines restricted what they could photograph, such as strangers in the community. They knew, in short, that the data were constrained. Because the purpose of the photography assignment was to help the participants articulate their perceptions, it is possible that the data gathered were not as expansive as they could have been had the photography guidelines been less strict.

It is impossible to know how the study would have been different had the youth participants had more input in its development and implementation. However, based on the feedback youth participants provided at the end of data collection, it is possible that more sessions would have been held outdoors in places that represented wellness to them (e.g., the park). Also, the data collection sessions would have been shorter.

Finally, the study could have been strengthened, especially given its YPAR focus, if member checking (Harper & Cole, 2012) had been incorporated. This was not possible with the youth due to IRB restrictions and the need for the research setting to proceed with other projects for their after-school program. However, one of the youth participants and his family attended the community meeting where the study and its findings were presented.

Overall, this study primarily taught us about the YPAR barriers that exist within universities. These barriers prohibit researchers' ability to engage youth as co-investigators in the research process. Consequently, we were aware of some of the study's limitations as a YPAR study prior to its initiation, given that youth could not be authentically involved in the research design. This chapter's final section expands upon this knowledge gained and shares recommendations on how to pursue a YPAR project to the best of one's ability, within the current constraints of the traditional research oversight infrastructure.

Final Reflections on YPAR

From a thorough literature review over the last several years and from experience in implementing YPAR, we found that there is great variation in the implementation of these studies. This variation is due not only to the education, experience, and intent of the researchers but also likely to a commonality often found among YPAR studies: *All* YPAR studies are inherently challenging.

Without exception, other YPAR researchers have communicated to the authors that in order to complete a YPAR study, the researcher needs to be flexible and willing to be co-learners (Minkler, 2000). This is a huge shift from the researcher as the dominant decision-maker. The lessons learned from conducting YPAR add to our collective understanding of what this kind of research entails, and what mainstream university researchers need to know and do differently.

The lessons learned in conducting YPAR can best be synthesized and categorized by steps in the traditional research process.

Study Conceptualization and Participant Recruitment

The study conceptualization and overall design of PAR studies are keys to not only collecting valid scientific data but also to utilizing those data for action. It is helpful for aspiring YPAR researchers to read as many YPAR articles as possible with examples of similar research goals. This will help the researcher understand the variety of potential methodologies that can be utilized and anticipate potential challenges. It may also be helpful to ask researchers with experience conducting YPAR to review one's research proposal and make recommendations for the design. Although it was impossible to do this for our own research due to IRB restrictions, it is ideal if the study can be codesigned and then implemented with youth from the population or community to be studied.

To recruit youth for the study (if the youth did not initiate the study themselves), it is helpful to have an "internal" research partner from the research setting who can help external researchers gain access to the youth. Youth engagement and interest in conducting PAR in partnership with adults is affected by the youth's interaction with adults in other settings. Consequently, it may take time to build a positive rapport and gain the trust of potential youth co-investigators.

University-Based Approval and Ethical Oversight

At this time, it cannot be assumed that the IRB and other groups and individuals with oversight authority for a study are familiar with YPAR (or PAR in general) and supportive of youth engagement in the research process. They also may not understand the value of youth engagement in the research process, and they may question the cognitive ability of children and adolescents to contribute to the research.

Therefore, researchers who conduct YPAR must be prepared to serve in an advocacy role for their study and also be able to educate others about the need for this type of research. Due to these potential barriers, it is also necessary to allocate additional time for the review and approval of the research protocol by the IRB, and to be prepared for a potential review by the fully convened board. It may be beneficial to request to attend the IRB meetings at which one's research proposal will be discussed to avoid several cycles of questions and answers with the IRB via written communication. The implications for doctoral students needing to complete a dissertation in a timely fashion are obvious but important to emphasize.

Methodologies

Researchers should use developmentally appropriate methodologies. *Developmentally appropriate* means methods that will actively engage and inspire youth co-investigators. In the case of the study investigating youth perceptions of wellness, photography was the data collection methodology, which the youth thoroughly enjoyed.

It is appropriate to adjust research methodologies for the youth participants' and coinvestigators' developmental level. However, these adjustments should be seen not as about "addressing developmental deficits, . . . but about addressing strengths" (Raby, 2007, p.47). In addition, it is common for high-school-aged youth to be the primary age group prioritized for YPAR projects. As we found through our studies, youth as young as nine (and likely even younger) can be meaningfully engaged in the research process and contribute to YPAR. Other researchers, such as Quiroz, MilamBrooks, & Adams-Romena (2014), also have effectively utilized photography and community mapping to engage elementary-school-aged youth in the research process and to obtain their perspectives on their local communities. PAR researchers should not discriminate based on age. Every young person has the potential to contribute knowledge and skills to these projects.

Dissemination of Findings for Further Action
Once the study is conducted and the findings are ready for presentation, it is possible that the adult researchers will be the ones invited to closed-door meetings to present and discuss the implications of the research. The first author experienced this on one occasion. Later, colleagues familiar with the principles of YPAR questioned her about why she did not fight harder to have youth present at a meeting that was designed to develop potential actions as a result of the findings. The first author acknowledges that as the adult and lead researcher, she should have worked harder in concert with community advocacy groups to have youth present for this particular meeting with decision-makers, despite their lack of support for this idea.

Unfortunately, it is not yet common practice to engage youth in decision-making that impacts their well-being, and this lack of engagement by adults is a silencing mechanism. The opportunity to present the findings of the study and participate in meetings within the community setting that may result in action as an outcome of the research is one way to help the youth participants feel ownership of the study and to be empowered within their community. This was a missed opportunity for the youth and the community. This missed opportunity is a lesson learned and a personal regret.

HOPES FOR FUTURE YOUTH ENGAGEMENT IN PAR

Our concluding reflections are provided not only to enhance the implementation of YPAR, but more important, to benefit the field of adolescent research and the well-being of this age group. Ultimately, the hope is that by increasing youth participation in research bearing on their well-being, health outcomes for this population will also improve. For this to occur, there needs to be greater appreciation for the youth voice by all facets of society, including the research community. It is also imperative that opportunities exist for youth to express their subjective experience for themselves, without reliance on researchers to capture the youth perspective through other parties (e.g., teachers, parents).

It would be beneficial to the research community and the adolescent population to support increased opportunities for youth to design and lead YPAR studies to benefit themselves and their peers. Hart's ladder of participation (1992) and other similar typologies are sometimes utilized to gauge the degree of youth engagement in projects. These tools can be used as an ethical check on the level or amount of authentic youth participation in research projects. Although it is not conceivable at this point that youth will be designing all the research projects that involve their well-being, it should be a goal that youth be given more opportunities to do so, with adults as supportive partners in the process.

Academic and practice-based organizations and journals should welcome, support, and actively recruit presentations and manuscripts that detail youth engagement in the research process, as well as the outcomes from this engagement. Youth collaborators on research projects should be given the opportunity to contribute to these methods of dissemination. For this to occur, research training, including human subjects training, should be developed and tailored to the cognitive abilities of this population to allow them to be coinvestigators grounded in the basic ethical principles of research.

YPAR would benefit if more organizations such as NACCHO and similar entities would issue statements and declarations in support of youth engagement in research related to their well-being. Aside from issuing statements, organizations with an interest in adolescent health and having the funding capability should modify their funding portfolio to include the support of YPAR projects, especially those in marginalized and underserved areas.

Although there is substantial work needed to advance the practice and scientific appreciation for YPAR, the PYD movement and growing support for this type of research are paving the path for more opportunities in this area. The field of social work, given its focus on research and practice, as well as its advocacy roots (Maschi & Youdin, 2012), is primed to continue to contribute to this advancement and to help lead it. Although this work is challenging, social work students should be encouraged to explore the opportunities to implement YPAR projects with the adolescent and young adult population. To alleviate the long-standing societal problems of our time, we must acknowledge the assets of youth—the default leaders of tomorrow, but the fully capable leaders of today. YPAR is one vehicle to allow youth to fulfill their leadership potential.

4

A Complex, Community-Based Participatory Action Research Design to Address Obesity in Young Children and Their Families

Janine M. Jurkowski, Kirsten Davison, and Hal A. Lawson

INTRODUCTION

This chapter describes an innovative research and development initiative called Communities for Healthy Living (CHL), which was structured to address childhood obesity among low-income families. CHL's leaders viewed childhood obesity as a complex and adaptive public health problem, one that overlaps significantly with social work because low-income preschool children and their family systems served as the target population. Our interdisciplinary research team consisted of social work, public health, and human development researchers. Our team implemented conventional qualitative and quantitative methods in tandem with community-based, participatory research (CBPR). CBPR typically is guided by a community advisory board (CAB). We structured our board in a unique way. Guided by a particular kind of empowerment theory, which we describe in this chapter, we viewed parents as experts. We added representative parents to the advisory board, and we also prepared parents and other community members to serve as co-researchers.

Results included a revision of a family ecological model for health-related behavior change (Davison, Jurkowski, & Lawson, 2011), enhancements to parent empowerment theory (Jurkowski et. al., 2014) and family-centered practice, and improved outcomes for targeted children and their family systems (Davison, Jurkowski, Li, Kranz, & Lawson, 2013). Salient details of the process follow, starting with the meaning and interdisciplinary significance of the child obesity problem.

TAKING STOCK OF THE CHILDHOOD OBESITY PROBLEM

Children establish obesity-related risk factors, such as poor dietary and sedentary lifestyle behaviors, at a young age. These behaviors are difficult to modify once habitual patterns are established (Campbell & Hesketh, 2007), and there are long-term, adverse consequences. Obesity early in life is a risk factor for chronic diseases such as obesity and coronary heart disease (Baker et al., 2007).

There is just cause to be concerned. According to the Centers for Disease Control and Prevention (CDC), 11% of children 2 to 5 years old were obese in 2011 (May et al., 2013). Contrary to the common belief that children will grow out of their "baby fat," children who were ever overweight during their preschool ages were greater than five times as likely to be overweight at 12 years of age than those who were not overweight during preschool (Nader et al., 2006). In brief, obesity prevention in early childhood may present the best chance to prevent childhood obesity and chronic diseases later in life (National Institute of Medicine, 2011).

Children in low-income and ethnic minority families are at increased risk of obesity (Anderson & Whitaker, 2009; R. Whitaker & Orzol, 2006). Both research studies and ecological theories (Davison et al., 2011; Stokols, 2000) suggest social and environmental factors account for this differential distribution. Minority children in particular are more likely to experience multiple social and environmental risk factors. These factors include stress, maternal depression, poor family functioning, single mother head of household, and lack of social support (Suglia et al., 2012).

In the same vein, availability and accessibility of grocery stores, parks, programs, and services and integration of services are also associated with childhood obesity risk. Low-income and minority children are less likely to have access to these resources (Davison et al., 2011; Sallis & Glantz, 2006; Wolch et al., 2011). When place-based social and economic disadvantage and single-parent stressors are included in the ecological realities of childhood obesity, the issue becomes a complex problem that suggests similarly complex solutions. Under these conditions, researchers need innovative models and interventions.

The Role of Parents in Childhood Obesity

In contrast to the dominant framing of the obesity problem as a children's problem requiring child-focused intervention, recognition is growing of the importance of parents' role in childhood obesity prevention from the beginning of life through adolescence (Dietz & Gortmaker, 2001; Morabia & Costanza, 2010). After all, parents are responsible for important environmental influences on obesity and health overall. For example, parents are instrumental in children's repeated experience with foods, ultimately influencing the dietary habits of preschool age children (Birch & Davison, 2001; Lindsay, Sussner, Kim, & Gortmaker, 2006). Later in their children's development, parents model eating behaviors that influence youth behaviors.

Furthermore, parental television viewing and physical activity behavior influence these same behaviors among youth (Andrews, Silk, & Eneli, 2010; Golan, Kaufman, & Shahar, 2006; Hingle, O'Connor, Dave, & Baranowski, 2010; Lindsay et al., 2006). Although school and community environments play a greater role among school-age children, parents continue to have a role in home food environment, physical activity, and television viewing (Lindsay et al., 2006; Whitaker et al., 1997).

The Knowledge Gap: Contextual Factors Left Out of Interventions for Low-Income Families

The popular idea of "translational research" derives from today's emphasis on reducing the gap between intervention research and practice (Glasgow & Emmons, 2007). Every profession is involved in this important work, and all are focusing on preventive interventions. Obesity researchers representing several disciplines are part of this pattern. They are striving to improve the relevance and effectiveness of prevention interventions, and with special interest in the transferability of interventions developed for a particular population in an almost unique setting to other populations and settings.

One new direction is especially salient. Leaders in the field of implementation science list the "failure to consider the community perspective in developing intervention strategies" as one of the main reasons for limited translation and dissemination of evidence-based approaches (Glasgow & Emmons, 2007, p. 417). According to Glasgow and Emmons, obtaining the perspective of the community in a way that gains the true perspective of that community is critically important. They recommend CBPR as one way to develop culturally appropriate and effective interventions (Israel, Checkoway, Schulz, & Zimmerman, 1994; Minkler, 2012; Minkler & Wallerstein, 2003).

Needs for innovative research and development initiatives that produce innovative, culturally competent interventions are evident in the places with multiple health disparities. Too frequently, interventions to address disparities among vulnerable populations such as low-income families do not achieve outcomes at scale because they fail to acknowledge and address family social, cultural, and economic factors, including how these factors are nested in community contexts (Davison et al., 2011). As mentioned earlier, the contexts of low-income families can include poverty and the availability and accessibility of resources in the community, such as programs and services, and the integration of services (Birch & Davison, 2001; Davison, Lawson, & Coatsworth, 2012). These contexts shape parents' knowledge and beliefs about obesity-related behaviors, parents' self-efficacy for promoting healthy lifestyles, exposure to chronic stressors through competing priorities, lack of social support, and lack of parental sense of control (Davison et al., 2011). They also limit the relevance of interventions to families and families' ability to participate in interventions that are more intensive.

It is noteworthy that most obesity interventions to date have focused on children, individually and together. Parental involvement in these interventions and intervention research has been limited to informed consent and consultation. This neglect of parents is paradoxical because they are the most knowledgeable members in their family systems (Jurkowski et al., 2013). They have important expertise about their family's needs, motivations, and resources for behavioral change (Morabia & Costanza, 2010). Parents also have insight regarding program relevance and feasibility. As such, parents' active engagement is important for the success of preventive interventions (Becker, Hogue, & Liddle, 2002; Dietz & Gortmaker, 2001). This need for active engagement is especially the case for low-income parents, whose children bear the burden of childhood obesity.

Possible reasons for researchers' neglect of parents and their expertise include researchers' deficit-based views of low-income parents and family systems and parents' lack of relevant professional training, as well as attrition (Prinz et al., 2001). When parents were included, they remained at the periphery of intervention design (Coleman & Hildebrandt Karraker, 2000; Fitzgibbon et al., 2005). All in all, in these designs, parents have been viewed as the mechanism for helping children, rather than as intervention priorities (Bathrellou et al., 2010; Collins et al., 2011; Golan, 2006; Golan et al., 2006; McCallum et al., 2007).

On "the parent side" of this research relationship, parents report lack of structural supports for participation, and they do not see the relevance of interventions for their life. Overall, parents also are reluctant to engage in research (Becker et al., 2002; Blom-Hoffman et al., 2008; Golan, 2006). In brief, there is an emergent pattern here, and it helps to explain reported low parental participation rates and high attrition (Prinz et al., 2001; Spoth et al., 1996).

Improving Parent Participation in Childhood Obesity Research

Given established links between parents' attitudes, knowledge, and behavior and children's dietary habits, physical activity, and screen-based behavioral factors associated with childhood obesity (Lindsay et al., 2006), it is timely to acknowledge parental expertise and incorporate parents' knowledge about their family's needs, motivations, and resources as well as their understanding of family dynamics and contexts that influence daily living (Morabia & Costanza, 2010). CBPR is one strategy for making this happen because it is predicated on the active inclusion of representatives from target populations as equals throughout the entire research process (Israel, Eng, Schulz, & Parker, 2005). In other words, this special research design helps to address issues of parent reluctance to participate and attrition, while facilitating their active engagement in research. It holds special promise for obesity-related research (Economos & Irish-Hauser, 2007).

A key progress marker is better relationships between researchers and parents. Acknowledging parents' expertise and treating them as equals in the research process may help break down historically hierarchical relationships between professionals (e.g., social workers, public health workers) and low-income families (Berge, Mendenhall, & Doherty, 2009). The CBPR process is structured to make this happen, while gaining parents' trust and facilitating their active participation.

Our research team added a special component to our CBPR. We aimed to facilitate parents' critical consciousness as one part of an overall empowerment strategy (defined later). In this study, critical consciousness is evident when parents are able to engage in critical reflection regarding the real-life factors that influence childhood obesity (Minkler & Cox, 1980), including parents' own inadvertent roles in contributing to it. More than analysis, this view of critical consciousness is based on parents' ability to identify salient solutions to complex problems like obesity and also to identify and address barriers to the implementation of conventional interventions.

Given the pivotal roles parents play in every aspect of young children's lives, it is surprising that, until recently, few published studies have explained how researchers engaged parents throughout the *entire* research process (Chomitz et al., 2010; Economos et al., 2007). Based on our team's literature review, CHL is the only known CBPR project that has emphasized the role of parents as experts and co-researchers in childhood obesity intervention research.

Communities for Healthy Living's Implementation of Parent-Centered Community-Based Participatory Research

The example of a parent-centered CBPR approach presented here takes place within the context of a study funded by the National Institute of

Minority Health and Health Disparities of NIH under the American Recovery and Reinvestment Act of 2009. The request for proposals prioritized CBPR in the development of interventions to address health disparities. What later was named Communities for Healthy Living, or CHL, was designed to structure a CBPR initiative focused on parents of low-income children. Parents and children in Head Start programs were targeted because it was easier to recruit, engage, and retain them in that they already were involved in these programs.

CBPR typically involves the development of a Community Advisory Board (CAB). Figure 4.1 provides a simple depiction. Because this boards vary, our approach to CAB membership provides an appropriate way to introduce the CHL story.

A partner community-based organization (CBO) is a very important part of the CHL story. From the beginning, our research team formed a partnership with the CBO administering Head Start in Rensselaer County, New York, the target county. Rensselaer County, in Upstate New York, was chosen because it has areas designated as Medically Underserved Areas. Here, 28% of all families with children under age 5 live below the poverty level, which is greater than the national average (U.S. Census Bureau, 2010).

Community Advisory Board (CAB) Membership

Parents

Research Staff   CAB   CBO staff

Community Reacquisition

Figure 4.1 CHL's Community Advisory Board.

The goal of the research project was to develop and pilot test a childhood obesity intervention for low-income families using a unique CBPR approach. Our approach was designed to actively engage parents across three phases: (a) partnership development, (b) community assessment and intervention development, and (c) intervention implementation and evaluation. The intervention targeted caregivers (mostly parents) with children in Head Start. We targeted parents/caregivers of approximately 500 Head Start children ages 6 weeks to 5 years old for a family-centered childhood obesity prevention intervention.

On the university side, our CBPR proceeded with an interdisciplinary academic team. Researchers had backgrounds in social work, human development, action research, childhood obesity, CBPR, and health disparities. Three of these researchers played leadership roles. Their respective methodological skills enabled the team to conduct mixed methods research. Methods included gold standard measures of childhood obesity, survey and other quantitative methods, qualitative methods, and participatory research strategies. This unusual diversity resulted in a methodologically strong and comprehensive study, one that is more expansive and rigorous than a typical stand-alone participatory action research (PAR) study.

From the outset, we, the CHL academic research team, viewed parents as experts. In fact, we prepared and supported low-income parents as co-researchers. We started with trust-building and relationship-building activities in an informal environment designed to minimize power, authority, and status differences. Our team made it clear that everyone was a teacher and a learner and also that we were committed to genuine parental leadership and empowerment. We emphasized that we firmly believed that parents provide unique expertise in their family realities, needs, and assets. We stated repeatedly that we highly valued their expertise and perspective and viewed it as essential for the childhood obesity prevention initiative. When we added parents to our CAB and informed them of the uniqueness of this approach, our actions spoke louder than our words.

Later, we recruited and prepared parents as co-researchers. These parents joined our interdisciplinary research team, and the team implemented multiple research methods for the development, implementation, and evaluation of the complex intervention.

CHL used participatory research methods to collect this knowledge and incorporate parental knowledge and expertise in the research.

A good example of this is the community assessment. Involved parents were co-researchers in that they were very involved in the development of assessment research questions, the identification of some of the assessment methods, and the recruitment and implementation of a mixed methods assessment. Parents also participated in regular research methods and PAR methods that CHL employed during the assessment (Davison et al., 2011).

For example, we recruited 16 parents to participate in photovoice research (Wang, 1999; Wang & Burris, 1997). This is a PAR tool, and it was introduced and described in chapter 3. The goal for using this methodology in CHL was to engage parents in the community assessment. This method enabled parents to record and later reflect on stressors in their daily life that impact their ability to promote healthy lifestyles within their family. Their findings later were incorporated into the intervention. In other words, parents' findings were consequential in the intervention design (Wang, 2003).

We also implemented windshield surveys (Barnett et al., 2007) with parents and organization staff for this same purpose—to engage the community in knowledge generation. Windshield surveys are a direct observation method. In the PAR tradition, windshield surveys involve community stakeholders. They narrate their own visual observations as they drive around a neighborhood with researchers. In this way, everyday people are able to provide valuable knowledge about neighborhood conditions, and this knowledge then informs a specific research topic (Barnett et al., 2007). Our parents' windshield survey findings influenced CHL intervention development.

Formation of the Participatory Decision-Making Body: The Community Advisory Board

To reiterate, we formalized the parent-engaged participatory process by creating a CAB. Although the term *advisory* has connotations that suggest power is not shared, our CAB shared power. Every CAB member was a part of the decision-making team and had a voice in striving to achieve a common goal.

By design, our CAB had a majority of parents. A local church reverend serving neighborhoods where Head Start families reside and a nurse from a local pediatric clinic serving over 60% of the Head Start families were also members of the CAB. Other community members recruited to the CAB included a representative from a local cooperative extension, a CBO board member, and other community agency representatives who lived within the community and were familiar with community resources. The CBO staff members of the CAB included the family and communities partnership manager for Head Start and program development staff. CBO staff members on the CAB, who worked directly with Head Start parents, recruited parents of children who currently attended one of the five Head Start centers and who also exhibited commitment to other Head Start activities.

Later the CAB expanded. More parents joined after participating in the research or hearing about the project through other parents. During the first two years of the CAB, the board consisted of 10 parents, 7 community representatives, the project coordinator, and the co-principal investigator (Jurkowski), who consistently attended meetings. Other parental and community representatives attended less frequently.

Empowerment Theory as a Guide

The unique combination of family ecological model and CBPR in this study led to the inclusion of empowerment theory. Once the CAB identified and interpreted family ecological factors, we recognized that CHL could not address all relevant social factors in a short period of time. CAB members then reached consensus on a short-term approach with longer term benefits. We decided that we could provide knowledge, skills, self-efficacy supports, and resources for parental empowerment.

Once we made this decision, we relied on empowerment theory along with the family ecological model to guide intervention development and evaluation. For example, we used a parent-centered CBPR process to create an empowerment philosophy for CHL. CHL leaders defined empowerment as the understanding of forces that affect life situations *and* the ability to gain power or control over these forces (Israel et al., 1994). In brief, this definition begins with critical consciousness but does not end there. Empowerment includes the ability to do something in order to gain relevant social supports and resources. Subsequently, we structured our CAB and our CBPR overall with the idea that parental empowerment was an important outcome.

This CHL conceptualization of empowerment merits more detailed examination because it includes multiple constructs. The particular construct employed at any given time depends on its use as a process measure or an outcome measure. The lead researchers anticipated that through the participatory process CAB members would gain several related benefits. For example, they would gain a sense of expertise (Morin et al., 2003; Schulz et al., 2003), network with each other and the research team, develop knowledge and skills (Granner & Sharpe, 2004; Laverack & Wallerstein, 2001; Schulz et al., 2003), and build self-esteem. At the same time, through critical reflection, power sharing, collaboration, and resource redistribution, the CAB parents and others serving as co-researchers would gain psychological and resource-oriented empowerment (Granner & Sharpe, 2004; Israel et al., 1994; Laverack & Wallerstein, 2001; Lawson, 2005).

With empowerment theory guiding the CBPR process, key elements emerged that made the parent-centered participatory research process successful. Figure 4.2 presents the CBPR process of the CAB. In this framework, we viewed the CAB in a unique way—as an intervention (i.e., a CAB process explicitly designed and conducted to be empowering).

We evaluated the CAB accordingly. We studied it as an empowerment structure designed to produce member equality, mutual respect

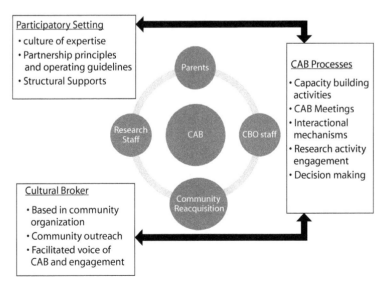

Figure 4.2 A Model of the CAB Participatory Process.

for each member's expertise, and a safe, welcoming, and open environment conducive to empowerment processes and outcomes. In the same vein, we strived to create a CAB that was conducive to relationship building and especially the development of cultural humility and competence, particularly among the professionals serving on the board. We describe these salient features next. We frame the discussion of the CAB's parent-centered CBPR process with the following key intervention elements: participatory setting, CAB process, and cultural broker. These elements are the key themes that emerged from the process evaluation—the CAB process to empowerment.

Participatory Setting
From the outset, the research team aimed to create an empowering, participatory setting for the CAB (Seidman, 2012). The team attempted to do so by (a) emphasizing an empowerment philosophy that embraced the parent-centered CBPR approach, (b) developing a vision and guiding principles that the CAB observed throughout its processes, and (c) providing structural supports to assist parental equal participation and acknowledge parents' social contexts, which need to be addressed to facilitate active participation.

Culture of Shared Expertise
The first CAB meeting during Phase 1 was essential for setting the participatory tone. Academic staff described the specific aims of the project, including the participatory approach, the role of parents as experts, the responsibility to the funder, and information about childhood obesity and its risk factors. From this important beginning the research team and organization staff made it very clear that parents were going to be equal in the research process as family experts who would be responsible for sharing their expertise in the research process just as the researchers and organizational members would share theirs to create a multidisciplinary team. This acknowledgment of parents' intellectual roles generated a sense of expertise, confidence, and responsibility to the project. This culture, along with an open, sharing environment within the CAB, fostered the belief among CAB members that they had a voice in the process.

Partnership Principles and Operating Guidelines
Many CBPR projects develop principles and operational guidelines to help clarify the terms of partnerships, codify expectations between

partners, and serve as guiding values for the partnership and research process (Levy et al., 2003; Minkler & Wallerstein,2003). Toward this end, CHL CAB members reviewed various other CBPR projects' partnership principles before beginning the process of developing their own during Phase 1 of the project (Partnership Development).

The CAB developed partnership principles during an 8-month period and approved them shortly before the end of Year 1. However, they served as a guide for CAB activities even prior to final approval. The CAB also decided to create operating guidelines to sustain active involvement in response to the inconsistent participation of some members. Several CAB members expressed frustration about time spent "updating those who do not show up." To address this issue, we obtained a sample of operating guidelines from a previous participatory project. Then we refined them to meet the needs of our CAB. Over a 3-month period, the guidelines were developed, revised, and ultimately approved by a unanimous vote.

Structural Supports for Parents and Other CAB Members

We put several structural supports in place to encourage consistent parental engagement. For example, we conducted CAB and most workgroup meetings at a Head Start center (where parents and children needed to be) immediately after the end of the school day. Parents were able to pick their children up from Head Start and attend CAB meetings in the same building. CHL paid Head Start teachers to provide childcare on-site. We also provided dinner to CAB members and their children at the beginning of CAB meetings, which allowed time for casual conversation and facilitated the development of equitable relationships among members. (Having diverse people with little or no history of previous interaction eat together and get to know one another over a meal is a recipe for success.) The provision of all such structural supports by CHL addressed low-income families' ecological realities, especially the multiple demands parents with young children confront daily, realities that otherwise often prohibit their participation.

This opportunity for community representatives, parents, and university staff to interact in an environment free from distractions helped build relationships. CAB members networked with one another and the academic staff, which led to tangible benefits for many members.

Examples include a parent talking to a nurse about her interest in becoming a nurse, and another talking to the researchers about programs offered at the university.

CHL leaders financially compensated members of the research team for their professional role as co-researcher. Organizational staff participated as a part of their professional role at the participating nonprofit organization. To reinforce the critically important idea that parents were experts and co-researchers who had professional roles on the CAB, CHL offered parent CAB members (and community representatives) $25 gift cards to acknowledge the time and expertise they contributed. CHL also offered these gift cards for parents who volunteered in research activities, such as recruitment, data interpretation, and intervention development and facilitation. Parents warmly received the gift cards. However, many of the active parents expressed that they would still have attended meetings regardless of the provision of gift cards because they felt ownership of the project and they wanted to see it through.

CAB Processes

Capacity-Building and Empowerment Facilitation

Although the CHL academic staff made it clear that parents were experts contributing to a multidisciplinary team, researchers' actions needed to demonstrate their commitment to parental expertise and validate the main idea of shared power with parents. Many of our CHL low-income parents had only a high school degree and often did not have professional job experience. So, they had to learn norms associated with professionalization and receive research training to participate equally in research study activities.

Although community organization partners were familiar with the roles and responsibilities of being a member of a committee or board, many of the parent CAB members did not understand the responsibilities that come with being a relevant member of a committee, nor did they have experience with the role of someone who has valuable knowledge and expertise. None of the parent and community members had experience participating in a research project. Therefore, it was necessary to provide training in a sensitive and respectful manner to build CAB member capacity for participation in the research process.

Partnership-enabling activities are actions for providing information, technical assistance, workshops, or other training sessions to support the work of the partnership (Fawcett et al., 1996). In the case of CHL, the academic researchers provided trainings and workshops that were relevant at different phases of the project. In Phase 1, CHL conducted trainings on research ethics, childhood obesity risk factors and behaviors, recruitment and interviewing skills, and effective communication. Some CAB members also learned and conducted qualitative data analysis. CHL academic researchers also taught some CAB members skills for survey design, data interpretation, and program evaluation.

In Phase 2, some of the CAB parents, the parent-facilitators for the parent program, participated in a multiday workshop. This workshop included teaching and group activities to facilitate parents' learning group facilitation, program coordination, and the educational components of the program. In Phase 3, CAB members requested training in fund seeking, grant writing, and stress reduction. Local experts in these areas provided training at CAB meetings. Further, a few CAB members participated in the dissemination of CHL and therefore were involved in peer-reviewed abstract writing and trained in PowerPoint and oral presentation skills.

CAB Meetings and Interactional Mechanisms

Due to the rapid timeline associated with our grant-driven project, CHL held CAB meetings twice a month for the first 6 months and then once a month for the remainder of the grant. In total, CHL held 25 meetings, including workgroup meetings, during the study. We created agenda items for the meetings with input from the academic staff, CBO staff, the project coordinator, and CAB members. The meeting structure varied depending on agenda items. Typically, it included a combination of small-group and whole-group discussions. The project coordinator primarily ran meetings, with the academic researchers facilitating when there was discussion and interpretation of data, and CAB members led discussion of specific agenda items. Although the project coordinator made efforts to have a formal leadership structure, none of the CAB members wanted to be an officer and take responsibility for the meetings.

CHL supplemented full CAB meetings with small workgroup meetings held at the CBO and at the university. At the beginning, CHL had smaller parent-only meetings prior to full CAB meetings to foster social connections among parents. Discussions in these groups focused on encouraging parents to think critically about factors that influence children's risk for obesity and to participate as experts and co-researchers. These meetings provided time for parents to talk openly about their experiences as parents and to ask questions without CAB professionals present. However, these meetings stopped at Month 3 because we noticed that parents had a strong presence at meetings and were active participants in the research process.

To facilitate planning and implementation, the full CAB was split into four small workgroups. Each had responsibility for one or more of the multiple aspects of the research. Most of the CAB members participated in at least one group, and some members chose to participate in multiple groups.

An ethics workgroup focused on the participatory process. A data workgroup helped guide the community assessment by developing the topics and interview guide for focus groups. This workgroup also conducted data analysis and interpreted findings.

At the same time, an education workgroup guided the development of materials for the parent program. A social marketing workgroup developed the Communities for Healthy Living logo, mission statement, project pamphlet, and social marketing poster campaign. All of these features were important for branding and were included in communications and CHL-sponsored events.

It was important to provide a social setting outside of meetings where the CAB members felt safe engaging in learning, expressing their viewpoints, and being involved in activities and decision-making (Seidman, 2012). A project policy was to include CAB members in as many activities as they were willing to participate in. Having the project coordinator based at the CBO fostered CAB involvement outside of CAB meetings. The coordinator was also able to be involved in the organization activities and link CHL activities within the organization. In addition to participating in CAB meetings, parents participated in day-to-day research activities alongside academic researchers as equal partners.

Figure 4.3 presents a summary of CAB activities and decisions, which varied across the three phases of the project. During Phase 1 of the project, the focus was partnership development. In Phase 2, the CAB fully participated in a thorough community assessment and the design of the CHL intervention. In Phase 3, the CAB focused its efforts

CAB Parent Involvement in CHL Activities and Decisions

Phase 1: Partnership Development

Activities	Decisions
• Establishing local partnerships • Formalizing CAB membership • CAB training in research methods and ethics	• "Communities for Healthy Living" name • Partnership Principles/Operating Guidelines • Creation of partnership MOU

Phase 2: Community Assessment and Program Development

Activities	Decisions
• Contributing in research team meetings • Participating in community assessment • Interpreting assessment results • Recruiting parents for assessment • Recruiting parents for parent program • Subcommittee designation • Identifying other community representatives	• Content of focus groups and PhotoVoice • Revision of BMI letters • Development of media materials • Design of a parent program intervention • Skills the program should develop • Essential program components • Identifying community issues to address

Phase 3: Program Implementation and Evaluation

Activities	Decisions
• Implementing program as Parent Facilitators • Providing feedback on community reactions to program components • Representing CHL at volunteer events and professional conferences	• Use of Parent Facilitators instead of professional moderators • Survey question revisions • Approval of dissemination materials • Seeking continued grant funding

Figure 4.3 CAB Activities and Decision-Making.

on program implementation and evaluation. CAB participation in all aspects of the research process led to a strong sense of ownership and satisfaction with having a voice (Jurkowski et al., 2013).

During the first meeting, the project coordinator engaged parents and community members in a discussion to obtain preliminary perspectives on childhood obesity. Prior to additional Phase 1 CAB meetings, we held smaller meetings with parent CAB members to build relationships, foster trust and communication, and reinforce the importance of their role. During the second and third meetings, the CAB worked in small groups with a flip chart and discussion questions to help them think critically about the determinants of childhood obesity among low-income families. CHL staff took notes during all meetings and workgroups to document discussions and decisions (Jurkowski et al., 2013).

Several benefits derived from the small-group discussion process. These included (a) increasing critical consciousness of childhood obesity among CAB members, (b) identifying social determinants of childhood obesity and other child health issues that were relevant to their community, (c) building relationships between CAB members and the CHL academic researchers and staff, and (d) operationalizing the expertise of parents by documenting their contribution to these discussions. During these meetings, academic researchers and the project coordinator trained CAB members in research ethics, childhood obesity prevention, interview and other research methods, and communication skills. All CAB members received an institutional review board (IRB) certification. (See Figure 4.2 for an outline of the specific activities in which CAB members participated and the decisions in which they were actively involved during Phase 1.)

During Phase 2 of the project, CAB parents participated in the design and implementation of the mixed methods community assessment, the interpretation, the dissemination of the results, and the development of the intervention and its evaluation. At least one staff CAB member of a partner organization participated in research team meetings during Phase 2. Several parents also participated. Their participation facilitated their involvement in the decision-making and research processes on a continual basis equal to that of research team members. For example, research team members, parents, and other CAB members worked together to develop research questions and develop and revise data collection instruments. CAB parents were very active in participant recruitment and some administered assessment tools. Parent members and one community organization CAB member were integrally involved in project problem solving and data collection planning for the assessment. Parents were careful to be inclusive of the entire CAB and at times suggested that members needed to bring certain discussions to the entire CAB. Parents sometimes presented discussions at CAB meetings.

Also during Phase 2, some CAB parents spent their summer investing many hours in intervention development (see Phase 2, Decisions, in Figure 4.2). In addition to being involved in the step-by-step design of the social marketing campaign and other educational material targeting parents, they also helped develop a 6-week parent program, Parents Connect for Healthy Families, and an intensive 4-day train-the-trainer session for parent facilitators. The program focused on increasing awareness of childhood obesity and its risk behaviors and providing communication, conflict resolution, stress management, and social networking skills, including how to leverage community resources.

During Phase 3 of the project (Program Implementation and Evaluation), four of the CAB parents participated as program facilitators. These Head Start parents participated in a 4-day training seminar along with other parents and then facilitated the administration of the parent program curriculum to their peers in the Head Start community. Engaging parents in both the design and leadership of the program ensured its relevance and was an important part of the participatory process. Other parents who joined the project as program facilitators subsequently joined the CAB after their experience working with the intervention.

The Importance of a Cultural Broker
The project coordinator for CHL reported to the principal investigators and also to the head of the local CBO. He was a key team member whose focus was to be a cultural broker (able to recruit, retain, and connect diverse families) and provide community outreach, including community-agency boundary-crossing work. CBO staff and the research team jointly interviewed candidates for the project coordinator position. In close collaboration with the university researchers who served as principal investigators for CHL, the CBO leader hired the project coordinator as a staff member of that organization. This arrangement proved to be an important feature of CHL because the coordinator was able to bridge the boundaries surrounding the CBO, the university, and the community, each with their respective cultures. The idea of a cultural broker derives from this work and the needs it addresses.

The principal investigators made a conscious decision to place the project coordinator within the organizational structure of the CBO to create project visibility at the organization, build relationships with organizational staff and parents, and facilitate organizational cultural exchange. The project coordinator's role of engaging parents early in the process was critical for building trust and fostering sustained participation. The project coordinator met with the parents to begin the relationship with the project and was accessible to them on-site in the community. Parents stated that the coordinator played an essential role by working with them when they felt they needed help with research translation.

Evaluation of the Participatory Process

Evaluation is an important component of a participatory process for several reasons. First, if a researcher conducts an evaluation throughout the study, early findings allow for adaptability and responsiveness to needs of the partnership. The evaluation may identify the need for modifications to the participatory process to ensure trust, satisfaction, and true participation in decision-making. For example, process evaluation may identify dissatisfaction among key stakeholders. With this kind of information, the other partners may approach these stakeholders to work through ways to improve the partnership for all partners.

Second, an evaluation allows the project to demonstrate an additional outcome. Demonstrating a successful partnership with parents and other community members that works effectively and leverages the assets and resources of all partners shows funders the group's potential for working on future projects. CHL's innovative parent engagement strategy is especially important because comparable initiatives have not been successful. Our evaluation was designed to demonstrate success and document the reasons for it so that others might rely on and enrich our work.

Third, evaluation can inform future parent engagement by identifying successful engagement strategies and lessons learned. Documenting and identifying successful strategies can also inform future partnership activities. Lessons learned can help future partnerships avoid wasting the time of key stakeholders, such as parents, and build stronger partnerships more quickly by avoiding pitfalls that may delay relationship-building or destroy a partnership's sustainability.

CHL's evaluation of the participatory process was originally a repeated measures quantitative design. The quantitative component was a closed-ended questionnaire to measure process and outcomes of participation. However, during Phase 1, CAB members expressed that they felt the survey did not adequately capture their experiences. They requested the addition of interviews, creating a mixed methods design (Creswell & Plano-Clark, 2011). CHL submitted an IRB amendment, which the Office of Research Compliance approved. This enabled CHL researchers to conduct in-depth interviews three times during the study and conduct a document review.

Thus, the participatory evaluation became a convergent parallel mixed methods research design to document the empowerment process and outcomes of participation in the CBPR process. A convergent parallel mixed methods research design is a common approach in which the researcher "collects quantitative and qualitative data during the same phase of the research process and then merges the results into an overall interpretation" (Creswell & Plano-Clark 2011, p. 77).

This mixed methods strategy was useful for multiple reasons. First, the small sample size of the CAB limited the statistical power for quantitative data analysis, but at the same time, averages and trends over time are informative for documenting the participatory process. Second, the repeated measures interviews provided in-depth data on process and outcomes at different times in the participatory research process. Furthermore, the direct quotes from qualitative interviews continued the participatory process, in which the actual voices/words and experiences of the CAB members are included in the evaluation results.

The participatory principles and operating guidelines provided a vision and guided the participatory process. The development of these documents was also a part of the participatory process. The ultimate benefit of this mixed methods strategy is that the data provided a more complete understanding of the empowerment process and outcomes.

The qualitative evaluation of the participatory process consisted of repeated in-depth interviews of CAB members, including research staff members who participated on the CAB. A CHL graduate research assistant interviewed community and parent CAB members twice over two years, after intervention development and toward the end of the project.

Moreover, a doctoral student interviewed university-based staff CAB members retrospectively toward the end of the project to derive CHL's theories of change. In addition, CHL staff analyzed the operational guidelines, partnership principles, and minutes of CAB meetings, which CHL generated throughout the implementation process. The document reviews at the end of each phase assessed CAB mission and values, CAB activities, and decision-making.

CHL researchers administered the quantitative questionnaire early in Phase 1 of the project and at key project points such as after intervention development, during intervention evaluation, and at the end of the active research project. The process evaluation measured trust, the feeling of having a voice, decision-making roles, and satisfaction with the partnership. Process measures were drawn from a survey shared on the Community Campus Partnerships website (El Ansari, 1999). The questionnaire also measured empowerment as an outcome of the participatory process, with the hypothesis that CAB members who participated throughout the research process would experience increased social networks, skills, self-efficacy, and resource empowerment. Partner organization staff and university researchers selected concepts of empowerment at the outset. University researchers sought existing measures from the literature. Researchers identified but modified them to document CHL's specific partnership processes. Additionally, researchers developed several new measures of empowerment for this study.

Preliminary Findings

A research assistant interviewed 16 CAB participants. We analyzed 33 documents in NVivo 8. We also conducted analysis of meeting and workgroup agendas and meeting notes to describe trends in participation in formal activities. Participation data are limited in that they do not document participation in many of the Phase 3 activities in which a self-selected group of CAB members participated in the evaluation of the project, including data entry and analysis or in the dissemination of findings.

Based on data that tracked attendance, there was consistent attendance among most members of the CAB. Although a core group of CAB parents and community members participated across all project phases, CAB attendance decreased over time, as there were fewer decisions to make. During Phase 3, the focus shifted to program implementation, and the majority of CAB parental involvement shifted toward participating as a parent facilitator or by helping the project coordinator administer the parent program or social marketing campaign. After the completion of the pilot intervention, the project focused on the evaluation. Fewer parents attended meetings, as there was less to do until the data were ready to present. Although some parents participated in data entry and other research activities during this time, many felt that this phase was not as participatory because they did not see a role for themselves.

CHL's Participatory Outcomes: Domains of Empowerment

Intrapersonal
• Self-esteem and self-efficacy
• Perceived control
• Perceived competence
• Awareness, knowledge and skill development

Interactional
• Ownership
• Collaborative/relational expertise
• Social support
• Access to resources
• Health-related critical consciousness
• Collaborative social capital

EMPOWERMENT

Research
• Enhanced awareness and cultural competency regarding obesity prevention
• New knowledge and protocols on CBPR implementation with CAB
• Improved quality of reasearch and measurement capacities

Behavioral
• Expressed self/voice
• Advocacy
• "Practice what you preach"
• Health behavior change

Figure 4.4 Emergent Outcomes of CAB Participation.

Not all CAB members shared this perception about lack of a role. The feeling resulted from the availability and interest in activities that were taking place during the different phases of the project. For example, one CAB parent attended two conferences and presented on CHL alongside academic researchers. An organizational member also participated in a conference presentation. In addition, interested CAB parents and organizational staff continue to participate in the development of abstracts, posters, and presentations for dissemination of the results. They are also actively involved in the development of additional research grant proposals.

The preliminary qualitative analysis of the CAB evaluation found four domains of empowerment—intrapersonal, interactional/relational, behavioral, and research—with many subdomains situating under each domain. The domains of empowerment are outlined in Figure 4.4.

Intrapersonal Empowerment

Parent CAB members in particular reported improvements in self-esteem and self-efficacy but also perceived confidence related to several factors. First, parents found that they felt more confident expressing themselves and stating their knowledge. Second, they reported an increase in understanding and awareness of childhood obesity and its risk factors. They also felt they had the competence to be able to identify and respond to their children's health needs. CAB members, especially parents, reported increases in knowledge, awareness, and skills related to childhood obesity prevention, child health promotion, and research methods.

The gains in knowledge and skills related to obesity prevention can directly influence parenting, and the knowledge and skills related to research methods can influence job prospects. Two parents reported that their skills in participant recruitment, facilitation of programs, and interviews helped them get their next job. In summary, intrapersonal empowerment, also called psychological empowerment (Zimmerman & Rappaport, 1988), was an important outcome of participating in CHL that is theoretically transferable to other aspects of an individual's life.

Interactional/Relational Empowerment

Interactional empowerment (Tigges, Browne, & Green 1998), alternatively rendered as relational empowerment (Christen, 2012), is a collective phenomenon, and it is especially salient to relationships among women. This form of empowerment among CAB members is salient because low-income families often experience social isolation and lack of social capital (Tigges et al., 1998). CAB members, especially parents, reported that by participating they gained social support from each other and bonded over having this collaborative experience. The interaction between community organizational representatives, researchers, parents, and the staff within the partner nonprofit led to an increase in access to resources for all involved, collaborative social capital, and an overall critical consciousness regarding the ecological contexts that families experience.

Oftentimes, "a blame the victim" undertone characterizes service agencies, and service professionals believe that low-income clients do not do enough to help themselves (Manning, 1997). Some CHL parents who were more successful at leveraging resources and maintaining a healthy lifestyle among their family members expressed this same perspective. By participating in this project, both parents and organizational members more clearly came to understand the ecological complexity of childhood obesity prevention and the adaptive nature of the poverty and its interaction with health among Head Start families (Davison et al., 2011). Over the course of our work together, blaming dynamics declined as strengths-based thoughts and interactions increased.

Behavioral Empowerment

In the context of CHL, behavioral empowerment is the ability to put action into gains in knowledge and skills. CAB members gained self-esteem and confidence through active participation and thus felt more comfortable expressing their perspective and having a voice. They felt that with the knowledge, skills, and comfort with having a voice that they were more able to advocate for their family. Also, once parents recognized they had the necessary behavioral antecedents, they felt they had to practice what they preached about healthy lifestyles and improve their own family's health behavior.

Research Empowerment

Researchers and community and parent CAB members experienced research empowerment in different ways. In this form of empowerment, increases in research knowledge, awareness, and skills improve research capability. In addition to CAB members' gaining experience and skills in research methods and implementation of intervention research, researchers also gained empowerment. Researchers' cultural competence for childhood obesity among low-income families increased because of the CBPR process. Researchers experienced increased awareness and knowledge of the complex and adaptive ecological factors that influence low-income families' ability to prevent childhood obesity and engage in health-promoting lifestyle behaviors. The participatory nature of CHL led to open discussion and data collection that identified deap-seated issues that answered questions about why low-income families disproportionately experience childhood obesity.

To summarize: Complex initiatives such as CHL are guided by and also facilitate "outcomes complexity." The four above-mentioned domains of empowerment provide a case in point. Figure 4.4 maps their relationship and provides summary details.

Final Thoughts

Research empowerment would not have occurred using traditional research approaches, because traditional approaches do not develop equitable relationships and trust between researchers and those researched—who typically are treated as "subjects" and "participants." Status differences and hierarchies are involved in this relationship, and they are especially likely to occur when marginalized and disenfranchised populations are involved.

On parents' side of this research relationship, oftentimes parents come to the research with a deep-seated belief that research does not generate a direct and beneficial outcome for those who participate in the research. Frankly, many do not trust the researchers. Consequently, parents and other community members are reluctant to invest and engage, and they may not put in the time and effort to help researchers learn with and from them. One result is flawed and skewed research. Simply stated, researchers often end up only studying the issues as they understand them, that is, from a selective and limited etic perspective.

CBPR, done well, and with critical consciousness as an explicit priority, can draw out hidden truths on the way toward development of better knowledge and more effective interventions. Researchers learn, adapt, gain new knowledge, and develop cultural competence alongside the participants. This is what occurred in CHL.

Owing to parent co-researchers, we university-based researchers were able to identify innovative "data truths" unique to the vulnerable families participating in CHL. These data informed changes in theory, helped to produce a unique parental intervention, and enabled the researchers to think differently and better about research designs and overall theories of change for CBPR.

For example, thanks to CHL's parent-led CBPR, the family ecological model was transformed to include more specific social and environmental contexts than the previous version (Davison et al., 2011). CHL's parental intervention became more expansive and multifaceted, including conflict resolution, communication skills, media literacy, and community resources (Davison et al., 2013). Furthermore, CHL's evaluation measures of specific constructs of parental empowerment reflect deep-seated understanding and knowledge revealed by the participatory methods and the CAB's reflection.

Although not the final word on these new research designs or the theories they test and articulate, CHL provides guidance and lessons learned for future researchers committed to addressing complex problems in real-world contexts, especially ones that have adverse effects on vulnerable people residing in variable, challenging places.

5

The Critical-Emancipatory Tradition of Participatory Action Research in Postdisaster Recovery Settings in the Global South

Loretta Pyles and Juliana Svistova

The outcomes of participatory action research are to be read in terms of historical consequences for participants and others involved and affected by the action people have taken, judged not only against the criterion of truth but also against the criteria of wisdom and prudence, that is, whether people were better off in terms of the consequences they experienced. (Kemmis and McTaggart, 2005, p. 322)

INTRODUCTION

Disasters such as hurricanes, tsunamis, and earthquakes carry the potential to create catastrophic situations. They are indeed wicked problems when the victims are already socially, economically, and politically vulnerable. Horrible, tragic events under any circumstances, their effects are especially harmful and hurtful in the Southern Hemisphere— known in some circles as the Global South. Postdisaster community work in the Global South is especially challenging because of looming threats and ever-present risks. Examples include the potential that outsiders have of exacerbating the situation; the limits that fragile infrastructures pose to productive work; and the cross-cultural barriers that inevitably exist between partners.

When one begins to contemplate working in any disaster setting, the ethical, theoretical, and logistical features of participatory action research (PAR) immediately gain practice relevance and importance. As with every kind of PAR, important practical questions must be addressed. Who is in charge? What assumptions guide the work? Whose voices need to be heard? What capabilities of participants need to be developed and nurtured, and how will the lead researchers progressively foster them? Whose questions matter most? And how will the research findings be used?

Beyond these PAR commonalities are important and unique contextual features of postdisaster work. Two such features are known as neoliberal policies and postcolonial politics. Neoliberal policies refer to a family of economic and social policies that in U.S. parlance have been called "trickle-down economics." In a word, these policies tend to favor growth opportunities for corporations over social welfare resources for people. Postcolonial politics refers to the intersectionalities of class, race, and gender that are always present when European White foreigners are engaged with communities in the Global South. Typically, these communities were reeling from the legacies of European imperialism and colonialism before the disaster.

Influential and powerful alone, in combination neoliberal policies and postcolonial politics structure a challenging context for PAR. Of course, we could attempt to ignore these realities completely, but local people demand and ethics require that PAR researchers in these contexts make a virtue of unraveling these realities. One of the purposes of this chapter is to articulate these histories, policies, and politics more fully, thereby clarifying why a unique form of PAR is required. In fact, PAR researchers who undertake this work are engaged in a form of transformative practice. One of the major ways in which this transformative practice is achieved is through researcher humility. Humility-in-action starts with the PAR investigator's bracketing of her or his own power and enabling grassroots actors to step into and build their own power.

Ultimately, the traditional boundaries between research and practice no longer hold. PAR becomes a special practice. In this chapter, we describe it as "critical-emancipatory PAR," and we emphasize its ethical dimensions and inherent challenges. We also describe how and why critical-emancipatory PAR aligns itself with social movements, especially social movement outcomes and processes and outcomes that seek to transform existing social relations. Critical-emancipatory PAR does this by giving primacy to the voices of the most marginalized people and continually interrogating issues of power within the PAR relationships.

We begin with a brief rationale for our claim regarding just how disasters in the Global South are a wicked problem. Next, we detail the histories, policies, and theories relevant to working in such disaster settings. Then, we articulate a model for working in the critical-emancipatory tradition of PAR, addressing key issues such as participation, roles, responsibilities, resources, and assets. We conclude with a brief case study of how the authors of this chapter employed critical-emancipatory PAR in postearthquake Haiti.

POSTDISASTER AS A WICKED PROBLEM

Disasters come with complexity, ambiguity, and uncertainty, together with a variety of perceptions and attributions. For example, some people consider disasters to be nature's or God's fury, and others claim that they can be traced to misguided international development policies or the uncritical development and implementation of production technologies (e.g., Bankoff, Frerks, & Hilhorst, 2004; Oliver-Smith & Hoffman, 1999). Other questions follow: Are disasters one-time events or historical progressions? Are they geophysical or sociopolitical phenomena?

In brief, interpretations of disaster carry complexity and uncertainty, and these interpretations matter in how we intervene. Seen as multilayered (economic, political, social, cultural, environmental), multileveled (individual, community, national), and multiphased (mitigation, relief, recovery, reconstruction), disasters are wicked problems. As with all manner of wicked problems, postdisaster interventions necessitate complex, interdisciplinary solutions. All such solutions must be both bottom-up and top-down. They also require empirical and theoretical advances to develop complex theories of action and change.

Such comprehensive knowledge development, integration, application, and theorization requires eclectic, flexible, and innovative research designs. PAR is one such design. Unfortunately, this view of the kinds of research needed is not self-evident. Oftentimes, disasters are treated, studied, and addressed as crisis events or technical problems with short-term, emergency solutions put forward without attention to local histories and culture, and more important, without genuine local participation (Berke, Kartez, & Wenger, 1993). Many of these approaches avoid the intricate net of complexity. They presume linear inputs and outputs that are conceived by experts and implemented from the top down (Schuller, 2007; Schuller & Morales, 2012), leaving out voice and choice for local residents.

Furthermore, the constellation of hardships that survivors of disasters bear includes basic needs like shelter, food and water, various physical and mental health issues, job loss and financial instability, adversities related to displacement and dislocation, and security and safety issues, to name a few. They cut across nations, classes, races, ages, and genders. And yet a long-standing line of research recommends a special perspective and attendant action orientation. *When disaster strikes, the most vulnerable, economically and socially marginalized populations living in precarious conditions, especially women and children, are the people who are affected the most* (e.g., Blaikie, Cannon, Davis, & Wisner, 2003; Dove & Huq Khan, 1995; Harwell, 2000; Luig, 2012).

In the global context, the place of disaster occurrence also matters. In other words, PAR researchers should be prepared to look for and act in relation to the plight of vulnerable people in particular places. On a macro scale, it is the developing world, also referred to as the Global

South, that bears the magnitude of disaster consequences the hardest. For example, Guha-Sapir and Hoyois (2012) found that in 2010 the economic impact of disasters was six times higher and the human impact was three times higher in the developing than in the developed world. This combination of vulnerable people residing in underresourced and undersupported places is noteworthy. The occurrence of disasters in the developing world adds yet another drop to the fountain of complexity. That is to say, in the Global South the compilation of global socioeconomic conditions and historic realities oftentimes causes (or at least exacerbates) the magnitude of disaster, not the natural hazard (earthquake, hurricane, tsunami, etc.) itself.

POSTCOLONIALISM, DEVELOPMENT, AND DISASTERS IN THE GLOBAL SOUTH

To presume to engage in any kind of action or research that may have the potential to transform social relations within the intricate web of the complexity of disaster recovery in the Global South, it is imperative that one have at least a basic understanding of both current and historical contexts. Indeed, by studying colonialist history, subsequent postcolonialist development projects, and the current imperialist practices of neoliberal globalization, one can begin to gain insight into the social production of disasters in the Global South. As this understanding grows, so does the practical relevance of social movements grounded in a critical-emancipatory tradition, including its centrality in postdisaster PAR.

In addition, as the critical-emancipatory tradition seeks to align itself with global social movements, PAR researchers take it upon themselves to learn about historical and contemporary forms of resistance and movement building. This practice is central to the process of becoming a competent PAR practitioner in such settings. In our view, one of the chief goals of this kind of PAR is to create spaces where local actors and their counterparts can work together to unravel the historical policies and practices that have led up to the current moment, thereby preparing the field so the group can co-create new practices that affirm the strengths and power of local actors.

Historical Context of Colonialism

Modern colonialism is a term that refers to a series of historical events and practices whereby European countries, including Spain, Portugal, England, France, the Netherlands, and others, "discovered," explored, and began to occupy countries and land in the Americas, Asia, Africa, and Oceania. The goals of these European powers were to expand their prowess economically, politically, culturally, and religiously. Beginning as far back as the fifteenth century, the peak of this activity is known as "high imperialism" (1870 to 1914). The imperialist activities of this era were connected to the Industrial Revolution and the desire of European powers to compete for markets and gain more natural resources (Allina-Pisano, 2009). The means to achieve these goals, more often than not, included violent and/or deceptive methods that resulted in losses of culture, dignity, and health for many indigenous peoples. Indeed, colonialism was a significant force in the global empire-building project of the major superpowers of today.

The colonization process included centuries of pillaging of natural resources, as well as trading of human resources in the form of slavery from Africa to the Americas and other parts of the world. The generations of people who survived colonialism faced tremendous loss and humiliation, as well as violence and death of loved ones. Local people were forced to adopt Christian religious traditions, foreign languages (French, English, Spanish, etc.), and the European cultures of their colonialist oppressors. Misery, poverty, poor health, civil wars, and environmental degradation in the Global South can all be viewed as legacies of the colonial era (Haslam, Beaudet, & Schaefer, 2009).

As the colonialist countries established outreach governments, some local actors became the eyes and ears of the mother government, through a practice known as "indirect rule" (Allina-Pisano, 2009). For example, during the "Scramble for Africa," these local actors would collect tax levies for the colonial state and receive a portion of the funds. "The overall effect was to strengthen existing cleavages or to create new ones in indigenous societies, with resulting social tensions" (Allina-Pisano, 2009, p. 39). In addition, these local actors were targeted for advanced education and became key candidates for the civilizing project, so that they could maintain the values and enforce the policies of the dominant country as well as serve as cultural interpreters.

Being in dialogue with these general themes of colonialist history as well as the specific histories of local contexts are vital activities of the critical-emancipatory tradition of PAR. Indeed, the practice of PAR becomes a way of deconstructing such histories and reconstructing a new set of practices. Moreover, Kemmis and McTaggart (2005) have suggested that the products of critical-emancipatory PAR need to be seen in terms of historical consequences, "in making and remaking of collective histories" (p. 597).

Throughout the centuries, there has always been resistance to this domination by those who were colonized, including individual micro-resistances to authorities as well as proactive collective actions such as community-building, storytelling of lost histories, and sharing of indigenous cultural knowledge that had been silenced or even forbidden, such as spiritual practices, music, and dance. In extreme cases, revolutionary overthrow was attempted, with an exemplary case being the Haitian revolution of 1804. Learning about practices of resistance in the Global South orients a practitioner to key features of critical-emancipatory PAR, strengthening practitioner knowledge of indigenous perspectives and needs and embracing local strengths in practice more authentically.

Social work has been implicated in this colonizing agenda, however unintentionally. Proposals to rectify and prevent colonizing social work increasingly are known as "decolonizing social work" (e.g., Gray, Coates, Yellow Bird, & Hetherinton (2013). Initially developed for social work practice and policy with indigenous peoples victimized by social exclusion, marginalization, and oppression, postcolonial social work also has special relevance for disaster assistance, supports, and resources, especially in the Global South.

Postcolonial Development and Disasters

The development project began around the middle of the 20th century after former European colonists ceded power to their subjects and the idea of the developing, Third World was born. From the perspectives of the former colonists, these developing, Third World countries needed to be "lifted up" so that they could begin to be on equal standing with developed, First World countries. This would mean bringing the proper infrastructure, technology, education, and economic development that would allow these countries to compete on the global market (Haslam, Beaudet, & Schaefer, 2009).

Thus, the humanitarian aid and development industries emerge based on implicit, firm assumptions about the inferiority of local actors and the superiority of outside actors. The practices of these industries are arguably grounded in the guilty consciences of Europeans and Euro-Americans who saw the negative effects of colonization, as well as the projections and fantasies that White people have about people of color and their needs. Indeed, the U.S. Peace Corps was conceived as a U.S. development project, which would allow, according to Representative John F. Kennedy, young college graduates to "find a full life in bringing technical advice and assistance to the underprivileged and backward" (cited in Leamer, 2001).

Oftentimes funded by foreign governments, multilateral partnerships, private foundations, businesses, and/or faith-based organizations, international nongovernmental organizations (INGOs) began to play major roles in postcolonialist development projects. These INGO actors were largely educated in disciplines such as anthropology, public health, and public policy. Social work has only recently begun to play a larger role in international aid and development work. INGOs such as Save the Children, the International Committee of the Red Cross, Oxfam, Doctors Without Borders, and many others have provided food, housing, medical care, education, and psychosocial support for vulnerable individuals, families, and communities in developing countries in humanitarian crises and for the sake of ongoing development.

Many have argued that these postcolonial development activities have largely replicated the modern colonialist practices of domination, Eurocentrism, and co-optation, albeit in more subtle forms (Gunewardena & Schuller, 2008). For example, in Haiti, a place referred to as "the Land of 10,000 NGOs," the groups of Haitians that tend to work with INGOs are referred to as "the NGO class." This moniker ascribes a whole set of problems and privileges that a PAR practitioner must anticipate and unravel.

Thus, when working in such a context, critical-emancipatory PAR researchers are invited to develop their personal knowledge of the complex layers of power as manifested in local-international partnerships, as well as local and global politics. Although presumably well intentioned, INGOs tend to be first and foremost accountable to their donor base and the agendas that they have set forth prior to even arriving in-country. This means that local actor perspectives may be silenced either subtly or not so subtly, breeding distrust of INGOs on the part of local actors in the Global South. As critical-emancipatory PAR practitioners enter the scene, cultivating awareness of such histories and realities and creating transparent environments becomes imperative in order for PAR to be a transformative activity.

Modern-Day Globalization and Neoliberalism

Globalization is not a new phenomenon. In fact, scholars consider there to be three distinct phases of globalization. The first wave of globalization was the colonization of Africa, Asia, Australia, and the Americas by Europeans dating back some 1,500 years ago. The second wave of globalization came through the Western ideas of "development" in the postcolonial period over the last 60 years or so. The third and current wave began in the mid-1990s through the "free trade" movement (Shiva, 2000). What is promising about this third wave of globalization is the deeper levels of interconnectedness among nations, including heightened multicultural awareness. However, neoliberal policymaking with its emphasis on the primacy of the free market endures, and it exacerbates disparities between the rich and the poor (Pyles, 2013).

The primary goals of neoliberalism are to cheapen the cost of the production of goods and to expand markets. Corporations and global financial institutions (e.g., the World Bank and the International Monetary Fund) have become key facilitators of this process, developing more power than national governments. It entails a phenomena known as the "race to the bottom" whereby multinational corporations move their factories to the places where they can find the cheapest labor, from the U.S. North to the U.S. South to Mexico to Bangladesh, and so forth, leaving in its wake the U.S. rust belt, unemployment, and sweatshops throughout the world (Pyles, 2013). In terms of overall impact, although many of these countries have a higher overall gross domestic product as a result of globalization, it has made a few people wealthier at the expense of driving down living and environmental standards of workers (Castells, 1999). With this context in mind, when a natural disaster such as a tsunami or nuclear meltdown occurs, the neoliberal recovery paradigm may actually contribute to the deterioration of conditions.

In a neoliberal context, disasters are seen as opportunities to advance capitalist goals. In fact, the conservative economist Milton

Friedman argued that capitalism thrives on disasters (Klein, 2007). After the earthquake in Haiti, Monsanto, a multinational agricultural corporation, donated genetically modified seeds to Haitian farmers, who refused to accept them, knowing that they would not be able to save them from year to year and that they would be forced to buy new ones from Monsanto each year.

In the case of post-Katrina New Orleans, many developers used the disaster as an opportunity to buy land and buildings at cheap prices to make a profit. As part of this postdisaster neoliberal project, the community became a laboratory for the privatization of public services, including schools, healthcare, and public housing. There is good evidence that the privatization of the public sector and the non-profit organizations that implement these policies play a critical role in advancing the neoliberal project (Pyles & Harding, 2012).

RESISTANCE TO OPPRESSION: SETTING THE STAGE FOR COLLECTIVE INQUIRY

The fascination with technical-rational approaches to international and local development work, including postdisaster recovery, perpetuates the idea that social problems can be solved linearly, relying on external experts and addressing symptoms and achieving predetermined outcomes (Haslam, Schaefer, & Beadet, 2009). All such approaches fail to address the origins and causes of social problems, and they silence inquiry into the history of colonialism and the political and economic causes of social ills.

PAR, in the critical-emancipatory tradition, promises something different. Critical-emancipatory PAR vows to provide a space for constituents to come together to develop an analysis of the social problems together. It is based on the critically important ideas that the answers to such questions are not readily available, and so the methods for intervention cannot be, indeed should not be, predetermined. Instead, all aspiring PAR leaders and social work practitioners must inquire into local histories of elites engaging in social control, violence, and subtler forms of silencing. This approach also requires that these PAR leaders and social work practitioners inquire into their own experiences with oppression, as well as the ways that they may benefit from oppressive structures; and it asks that actors analyze existing social interventions and the ways that they have been successful and the ways that they have failed.

These activities of inquiry are key components of the PAR process in postdisaster contexts. They always are conducted within the collective, as a group process.

This process is salient for a variety of reasons. First, although the impact of oppression and the effects of social problems on people's individual lives are very important to understand, it is equally important that members of the group hear each other's stories and histories, engender solidarity among themselves, and develop a shared analysis of their particular social situation.

Second, when PAR philosophical and practical roots in the Global South are emphasized, PAR practitioners must be deeply aware of collectively oriented cultures and activities. In other words, cultural differences matter, and they must be a point of departure for PAR leaders. After all, Eurocentric social practices tend to favor the analysis of elite actors (in the development and humanitarian aid environment, this tends to be program managers and the executives of INGOs). Responding to histories of colonization, and embedded in indigenous culture, local actors often demand collective analysis, problem-solving, and evaluation.

Third, PAR leaders must anticipate an ever-present threat to the integrity of their emancipatory, empowerment-oriented agenda. This threat is a function of working in a neoliberal, postcolonial context whereby the layers of social hierarchies between insiders and outsiders, as well as among local actors, are highly relevant. Those actors who are in the middle of the hierarchy are more prone to adopt and accept the agendas of the elite at the expense of the agendas of those below them; this is a form of co-optation.

Thus, local actors, that is, "the NGO class," hired by international NGOs, may become co-opted, taking on the values of their supervisors and funders. Although such individuals are presumably hired to serve as cultural interpreters and would ostensibly value collectivity, this is not always the case. Such cultural interpreters may be resistant to address such issues and engage in movement work that would subvert the dominant paradigm due to fear of losing their place in the social hierarchy.

Fourth, collective approaches to problem-solving in PAR projects are necessary because more people can bring greater diversity of perspectives, not just diversity from the purse string holders, but diversity within the community. This is related to the previous point whereby social hierarchies within the country can play themselves out quite easily so that local elite males become the sole voices of change. Thus, older adults, youth, women, people with disabilities, people from a variety of religious backgrounds, and others bring critical perspectives.

To conclude, a social work PAR researcher needs to develop a profound understanding of postcolonialism, development, globalization, and neoliberalism as critical-emancipatory PAR was, in part, conceived as their remedy. In postdisaster contexts, such knowledge is especially critical not only in terms of self-aware, socially just, and anti-oppressive PAR practice but also because the compilation of these development processes cannot be separated from the mere natural causes of disaster.

PHILOSOPHICAL FOUNDATIONS OF THE CRITICAL-EMANCIPATORY TRADITIONS

Mainstream practice of research is one of many exclusionary elitist social practices performed by the knowledge holders toward research subjects. The issues of power inequality and exclusion surface very clearly in the conventional research enterprise. This dynamic is especially pronounced in postdisaster contexts, wherein the majority of the research is conducted *on* the developing world *by* researchers from the developed nations (Norris, Galea, Friedman, & Watson, 2006). In this approach, the people affected by disaster are human subjects, and this expert knowledge and research expertise belong exclusively to credentialed researchers from the developed nations.

In contrast, PAR has emancipation at its foundation. The critical-emancipatory tradition of PAR serves to reclaim the power of the people by centering them in the research and social change process. This special tradition is influenced by the philosophical foundations of Marxism, feminism, social constructionism, and popular education of Paulo Freire. At its core, critical-emancipatory PAR emphasizes alternative views of epistemology (whose knowledge counts), power (who participates and how), and social change (to what extent social relations are made more equitable). It behooves all researchers, especially doctoral students preparing for a research career, to address these fundamental issues and avoid the tendency to accept the dominant positivist view of research as the only alternative. For the social work doctoral students who are still fresh as practitioners but are rapidly budding as social scientists, discovering this alternative notion of the research enterprise may be liberatory in and of itself.

We emphasize four philosophical foundations that underpin critical-emancipatory PAR. First, any social change activity must acknowledge the influence of 19th-century philosopher Karl Marx and the Marxist tradition, as this philosophical tradition has brought forth an influential analysis of the nature of relations between the "haves" and the "have-nots." By cultivating class consciousness, as well as offering knowledge about the exploitative nature of capitalism and, in the contemporary context, neoliberal globalization, vulnerable actors can apply this knowledge in their own lives, organizations, and communities. Later critical theorists in this tradition, such as Antonio Gramsci, argued that society is hegemonic, that is, people come to believe in the naturalness of and acquiesce to oppression, which is dependent on the daily reinforcement of the relations and conditions through the media, the workplace, and economic arrangements (Kaufman, 2003; Pyles, 2013).

The good news is that resistances to oppression, big and small in scale, occur in every instance in the hegemonic context. Critical-emancipatory PAR is an example of resistance against the positivist tradition dominating the research enterprise of today, as well as an act of opposition to the imperial practices of the past.

Thus, the critical-emancipatory framework of PAR owes allegiance to this kind of "critical" inquiry into social relations and its winners and losers (Kincheloe & Mclaren, 2000). As Marx aptly said, the goal is not simply to interpret the world, the point is to change it (cited in Pyles, 2013). Thus, the social analysis that results can propel actors toward emancipatory actions and social change activities such as PAR. The Freirian, feminist, and social constructionist traditions all provide useful tools for engaging in such analysis and moving forward to effect change.

The second philosophical foundation underpinning critical-emancipatory PAR is popular education, pioneered by the Brazilian educator Paulo Freire (2000). The key premise of popular education, or pedagogy of the oppressed, is that structural and cultural changes may be achieved through consciousness-raising whereby people become aware of how their thinking serves to preserve structures that work against their best interests. Opposed to injecting knowledge, popular education promotes reflection and social analyses that lead to awareness of a system's workings and further action upon it. Freire (2000) believed that it is through participation and action that people become empowered and indeed reclaim their power. Originating in the Global South and removed from the Eurocentric vision of social realities, Freire's philosophy of pedagogy and social transformation is an important contribution to PAR.

Third, feminism traditionally is concerned with gender inequality and female subordination in society. Feminist thought today has evolved beyond the issues of women and gender. It is concerned with power and transformation of societal structures and relations. It stands against top-down, hierarchical relations and opposes the imposition of dominant norms, rules, and ways of being. Fook (2002) stated that feminism of today is concerned with the epistemic effects of social stratification, that is, how cognitive and social authority gets distributed and whose assumptions are taken for granted. Feminist practitioners advocate for visibility and voices of those on the margins of society. Thus, feminist community-organizing principles (like critical-emancipatory PAR) affirm community involvement, collective problem-solving, process as part of the goal, consciousness-raising, consensus, cooperation, collaboration, coalition-building, unity and wholeness, and praxis (Education Center for Community Organizing, n.d.).

In addition, PAR operates from the "personal is political" standpoint that originated in feminist thinking. In practice, this means that by providing safe spaces for people to give voice to their experiences of oppression and liberation through group process, consciousness-raising, and shared analysis, what was once an isolated, individual experience now is understood as a shared experience that can politicize the group and move them toward solidarity actions. These feminist organizing characteristics have clearly influenced critical-emancipatory PAR philosophy and practice. Acknowledging the feminist influences on PAR is especially critical in the context of the Global South, where gender inequality and exclusion of women from the public sphere are still common and rampant practices.

Fourth, critical-emancipatory PAR also has roots in social constructionism, a postmodern epistemological perspective that raises questions about the essence of knowledge and social reality, how we come to know it, and how we produce, express, and communicate it (Rodwell, 1998). It essentially proposes that there are multiple realities and ways of knowing and that all knowledge counts as valid. If all meanings are encountered as potentially possible and valid, through dialogue, reflexivity and reflective practice, and shared exploration of issues, a new comprehensive reality can be created (Rodwell, 1998). Social constructionists also suggest that this may disrupt dominant constructions and lead to abandonment of the role of expert and a power shift can potentially happen. The validity, legitimacy, and inclusion of all knowledge, expert or indigenous alike, are key attributes of critical-emancipatory PAR.

THE RADICAL TRADITION IN SOCIAL WORK AND ITS CONNECTIONS TO CRITICAL-EMANCIPATORY PARTICIPATORY ACTION RESEARCH

Although social work expounders have strong rhetoric about empowerment, social justice, and other like aims, scholars have criticized the profession's depth of understanding and actualization of these ideas (Pyles, 2013). Indeed, the social work profession tends to operate within mainstream institutions and more commonly utilizes traditional structures and methods (firm professional-client divides, hierarchical organizational charts, and linear, outcome-oriented interventions) as compared to those of social movements (flattened organizations and processes, consensus-oriented approaches, etc.).

However, social work does indeed have its own radical tradition that is commensurate with the critical-emancipatory tradition (Pyles, 2013; Reisch & Andrews, 2002). Through its involvement with unions during the Progressive era, its proactive responses to U.S. Senator Joseph McCarthy's "Red Scare" and witch-hunt for communists in America, and its role in the development of the National Welfare Rights Organization, social work has indeed aligned itself with social movements and sought to change the status quo.

The transformative community-organizing model (Pyles, 2013) and the feminist community-organizing model (Joseph et al., 1991) are examples of social work approaches to community organizing that embrace critical-emancipatory PAR as one of many organizing tactics. These approaches affirm the importance of collectivity, a critical stance, intersectionality, self-inquiry, and the primacy of process over outcomes. In addition, social work academic journals such as *Journal of*

Progressive Human Services (formerly called *Catalyst: A Socialist Journal of the Social Services*) and *Critical Social Work* serve as repositories for the knowledge and wisdom accumulated through this progressive tradition. Thus, scholar-activists who align themselves with the radical social work tradition are aptly suited to participate in critical-emancipatory PAR projects.

WORKING IN THE CRITICAL-EMANCIPATORY TRADITION OF PARTICIPATORY ACTION RESEARCH

Even though the formal colonial-imperial powers of the Global North are long abolished, the entrenched relationships of inequality have traveled in time and mapped onto the new regimes of dependency in the Global South. Today, the processes of development, globalization, and neoliberalism all continue to construe the terrain of top-down relationships, relegating people to the periphery of the political and economic global system. In this context, social work researchers are obliged to adopt roles and responsibilities that break through social injustices and exploitative practices of the past.

To this end, participatory action researchers of the critical-emancipatory tradition engage in research as a social practice. This conception of PAR goes beyond mere research practice with a goal of finding, understanding, theorizing, acting, and transforming. Intertwined and interrelated with others in the social world, PAR researchers seek to reflect on their acts of communication, production, and social organization (Kemmis & McTaggart, 2005). This stance requires researchers to give up control and power, embrace spontaneity, and allow the experience to unfold, while being nonjudgmentally present in acts of joint transformation with the collaborators.

This tradition of PAR is a part of a larger existence for the researcher. That is, PAR is a way of being in and with the world, one that proceeds beyond technical skills. PAR thus is holistic because it aligns with the social work investigator-practitioner's identity, whereby who she or he is equals to what she or he does, and vice versa. Development studies scholar Marja-Liisa Swantz (cited in Reason & Bradbury, 2001, p. 1) explains her own stance: "I do not separate my scientific inquiry from my life. For me it is really a quest for life, to understand life and to create what I call living knowledge—knowledge, which is valid for the people with whom I work and for myself."

Further, resistant and transformative acts of inquiry in the critical-emancipatory tradition of PAR oppose the conventional research enterprise. In this view, the conventional research approach is a hegemonic social practice with the potential to marginalize, oppress, and disempower people. In other words, conventional research co-creates and reinforces a particular kind of social reality, one dominated by inequality.

Critical-emancipatory PAR radically challenges and changes this conventional researcher role and the effects of conventional research. With PAR, the research makes no pretense about social distancing in service of objectivity. Instead, the researcher is explicitly embedded in social reality. With PAR, the investigator is immersed in an existential practice of research, which paves the way toward the social world we want to belong to, the "world worthy of human aspiration" (Reason & Bradbury, 2001, p. 1).

As Kemmis and McTaggart (2005) explained, the emancipatory aspect of PAR lies in breaking through the unjust social structures, and its critical aspect lies in the breaking through and recovering from the constraints of social media (language, modes of work, and social relationships of power) that are all created throughout history. Working in the critical-emancipatory tradition of PAR therefore involves indigenous epistemologies (conceptions of what counts as knowledge), truly participatory process and ultimately transformation of social practices and relationships. Such an approach to PAR is obstinate about changing "particular practitioner's particular practices" and changing the "irrational, unjust, alienating, or unsatisfying" practices of groups of people through which they interact in a shared social world (Kemmis & McTaggart, 2005, p. 277, 283).

PAR is structured to create a communicative counterspace, that is, social settings where marginalized, vulnerable, and oppressed people are honored, respected, and enjoy voice, choice, and genuine decision-making power and authority. Under these conditions, participants reach intersubjective understanding and arrive at fundamental consensus, albeit experiencing in the process conflict, disagreement, and the power of better argument (Kemmis & McTaggart, 2005).

With this kind of PAR, research is not merely about the cold, hard facts generated by dispassionate researchers. As an integral aspect of communicative acts, emotions and feelings are brought to the forefront of this transformative process as alternative ways of generating and scrutinizing participants' knowledge of the social world. Such an unusually welcoming stance in the research enterprise serves to democratize scientific practice, to tap into the affective self of the participants, and to consequently motivate their political agency (Kemmis & McTaggart, 2005). Carried to its farthest reaches, engagement in such practice of PAR can become a truly therapeutic and transformative experience (e.g., Lykes, 2013).

Figure 5.1 Toward a Theory of Action in the Critical-Emancipatory PAR Tradition including the Four Key Dimensions of Context, Research, Action/ Transformation and Participation.

In the tradition of action science, in Figure 5.1 we offer a theory of action model as it relates to the practice of PAR in the critical-emancipatory tradition. As articulated in the model, the critical-emancipatory tradition of PAR is conceived of as a social practice. At the same time, PAR provides a space of resistance to the dominant approach to research with its hegemonic ways of relating to others (hierarchical), knowledge derivation (positivist), and/or professional interventions (top-down). It invites the inclusion of marginalized and silenced voices that are largely unrecognized by the dominant positivist research paradigm.

In this visual representation of the process of critical-emancipatory PAR, the circle symbolizes a holistic, yet recursive, ever-evolving and transient process of PAR. In this approach, all four elements (context, research, participation, and action) are strongly connected. This model also suggests that the contexts with embedded conditions, circumstances, and intentions set the stage for PAR as emancipatory social practice. Each of the four elements specifies the key procedural features that define and distinguish critical-emancipatory PAR from other approaches to PAR. We theorize that at the center of critical-emancipatory PAR are the issues of what counts as knowledge (epistemology), whose and what knowledge counts (power), how such inclusion of all knowledge is ensured (participation), and what social changes ensue as a result (emancipation and action). In the following section we describe the nuts-and-bolts of the model.

Empowerment, Participation, and Decision-Making in Participatory Action Research Projects

This kind of PAR is designed to democratize scientific practice and reconstruct historically created social relations. Consequently, citizen participation and people-driven processes are set in the forefront of critical-emancipatory PAR. The "participatory" part of PAR is especially important. However, not all participation is alike, and participation is not automatically empowering. Power and control sharing, the nature of decision-making, and the depth of engagement essentially define the level of ownership and participation.

Unfortunately, labels of inclusion and participation are not always authentic. In fact, many interventions in the Global South have been found to be manipulative and largely tokenistic in essence (e.g., Schuller & Morales, 2012). Manipulative participation stands for pretentious representation of people from the grass roots with no true power in actuality, whereas tokenistic participation represents the inclusion of people into the prearranged agendas solely for consulting or informing purposes (Cornwall, 2008). Although appropriate in some contexts, such erroneous views of and (oftentimes purposefully) deceptive manipulations of "participatory" practice can do harmful service to the people in the Global South, thereby exacerbating problematic postcolonial politics.

When critical-emancipatory PAR provides the evaluative framework, all such manipulative and tokenistic approaches to participation are rejected as colonial expressions. These approaches also are viewed as largely invalid and ineffective for empowerment and transformative purposes.

Critical-emancipatory PAR therefore strives for true participation and citizen power, perpetually denied to the people in the Global South. Citizen power and participation are seen as a human right, not a mere means toward the research goal (Cornwall, 2008; Kemmis & McTaggart, 2005). Consequently, the meaning and practice of participation in PAR is not equated to mere attendance and presence at the meetings. Rather, meaning and participation are measured in the quality of member engagement and power sharing, the depth of discussions, the extent and importance of contributions, the level of collaborative learning, knowledge sharing and generation, and consequent actions taken to effect change. This means, for example, that research questions are co-created by the entire research team, stemming from the articulation of the lived experiences of local actors, as well as a shared social analysis of these experiences developed by the whole group. Here we see all four elements of our research model at work and forming a productive synergy. The *context* and *participation* of actors set the stage for and create the *research* questions that will move actors toward *action/transformation*. These descriptions of the participatory process align with feminist organizing principles and the Freirian idea of social transformation.

As has been established throughout this chapter, a critical-emancipatory approach to PAR seeks to transform oppressive social relations, practices, and historical consequences that accrued due to colonialism, failed development projects, globalization, and neoliberalism.

The democratic, inclusive, participatory process of PAR serves to satisfy such an objective. Building on the lived experiences and tacit knowledge of the collaborators, the overarching goal of PAR is to arrive at critical understanding of social reality, to develop skills and capacities for action, and to consequently gain control over their own environments. Equipped in this way through the critical-emancipatory PAR process as presented in the model above, in the final, definitive step, collaborators take action toward transforming unjust and oppressive relations and conditions that they simultaneously co-create and are shaped by (Freire, 2000; Kemmis & McTaggart, 2005). Herein rests the empowering process and the empowerment goal of the critical-emancipatory PAR.

ROLES AND RESPONSIBILITIES OF SOCIAL WORK AND OTHER PARTICIPATORY ACTION RESEARCH RESEARCHERS

The roles and responsibilities of social work PAR researchers are defined by ethical and moral obligations as makers of history. The roles and responsibilities of action researchers in the critical-emancipatory practice of PAR extend long beyond "thinker" and associated cognitive and analytic functions of the distanced social analyst. In the same vein, the PAR investigator's project leadership, coordination, and facilitation do not end with the implementation of the research.

All the while, the PAR researcher proceeds with a special orientation toward the work, the people, and the place. Detached from the imperialist mission to save, and to develop or to normalize in hegemonic traditions, the researcher of the critical-emancipatory PAR tradition manifests humility. This entails giving up control, embracing serendipity, and allowing the experience to unfold. Bringing in the affective and vulnerable self, the researcher takes on a role of an equal participant or collaborator eager to learn from others, bring awareness to his or her own experiences with privilege and oppression, and to change one's being in the world (Behar, 1997).

The PAR research thus must be both a competent social scientist and a dynamic practitioner. Practice skills include setting the stage for developing rapport, building trust and relationships, and managing chaos, conflict, and distress (Reason, 2011). In these ways, the social work critical-emancipatory PAR practitioner utilizes his or her generalist social work practice skills, competencies, and sensitivities—especially group practice skills. Capable to invoke emotions and withstand emotional tensions, the PAR practitioner is also skilled to turn such situations into teachable moments and redirect them toward a potential for personal and collective transformation. With the close and prolonged collaborative relationships, action researchers require a well-developed set of cultural competence skills. Part of the cultural competence in critical-emancipatory PAR is the awareness and critical standpoint of the PAR researcher's own embodied privilege, beliefs, values, ways of being and doing, and passions. As has been explained in detail, when engaging with the Global South, the culturally competent PAR practitioner understands and draws on the importance of the collective as a cultural asset. Yet, a PAR researcher also needs to develop awareness and understanding that cultural norms and practices do not always work in the best interests of the most vulnerable, such as in a culture where women are viewed as second-class citizens. There is a very likely chance of reproducing and perpetuating deeply entrenched social hierarchies and exclusion of marginalized people. To this end, a PAR researcher respects cultural norms, but understands that culture is socially constructed and purposefully fosters the inclusion of historically excluded voices. Indeed, it is the centering of women and marginalized people in the process that differentiates critical-emancipatory PAR from traditional forms of PAR.

For example, women, who tend to be marginalized and oppressed throughout the globe as a function of patriarchy, but particularly in the Global South, will be especially vulnerable after a disaster. Indeed, the research reveals that women are more likely to be injured in disasters, have more caretaking responsibilities and are particularly vulnerable to both intimate and stranger violence after a disaster (Fordham, 1999). If patriarchy was the norm before the disaster, the risk is that even the best-intentioned PAR practice will fall prey to it. The role of the PAR practitioner is to foresee and prevent further exacerbating it, and indeed, in the critical-emancipatory tradition, to seek to transform it. Ensuring equal representation and inclusion of women, therefore, is a critical aspect of culturally aware transformative PAR.

In addition, a component of cultural competence, as we see it, is the action researcher's ability to translate the culture of academe/research and that of community collaborators and to bridge them in the act of joint transformation. A part of such an endeavor is the deliberate use of ordinary, inclusive language in seeking to flatten the hierarchies created by the use of professional language and specialist discourses (Kemmis & McTaggart, 2005). The ability to navigate through and resist the restrictive Western research system (e.g., bureaucratic institutional review board processes) also adds to the social work researcher's skill set of cultural competence.

BUILDING COMMUNITY CAPACITIES AND RELATIONSHIPS FOR PARTICIPATORY ACTION RESEARCH

Building relationships and community capacities for PAR is closely related to sustainability of the research as development effort. Providing research trainings, ensuring participatory discussions, encouraging cultural consultation regarding data collection procedures, and hiring local community members as researchers all work toward the capacity-building goal. Explaining the uses, utility, and process of research in detail and engaging local community researchers builds trust and better ownership of research initiatives. Also, this can serve as a means toward long-term sustainability. For example, the data collection tool can be used in future community research initiatives, and the findings can be used for advocacy and lobbying purposes or professional trainings for international aid organizations. In the Global South, where indigenous communities have been used and abused by the outsiders, such thorough explication helps to transcend the view of researchers as opportunists replicating colonial legacies in modern times.

For these same reasons—transparency, genuineness, and loyalty of action—researchers define their engagement and relationship-building with the collaborators. They are clear and honest upfront about who benefits and what the possible deliverables are. They fully acknowledge and make transparent the contribution of the collaborators. They also take it as a moral and ethical responsibility to disseminate the findings of the research back to the community of collaborators so that they are informed as to how their information was used, and so that they can further use this evidence for bettering their conditions. PAR researchers do not simply disappear once the research project is over; they stick around for further collaborative projects or make themselves available per community request.

FACILITATORS, RESOURCES, AND ASSETS NEEDED FOR PARTICIPATORY ACTION RESEARCH

Transformative research, empowering processes, and relationship-building all require significant resources and institutional support, as well as specific values and virtues on the part of individual actors. Actors in the developing world may believe that the researcher has an unlimited source of funds, so it is important to communicate about the budget that is available for the project, including ongoing updates about spending and any new potential sources of funding. How much funding is available is less important in the critical-emancipatory tradition than the group's relationship (discourse, decision-making, etc.) to the funding. For example, in some cultures of the Global South it might be more sustainable, empowering and culturally appropriate to distribute research participant rewards to an entire community for collective purposes, rather than to each individual research participant in the community (e.g., Svistova, Pyles, & André, in press).

It is imperative that the research team has the support of the leaders of their respective institutions and organizations. As a faculty researcher, it can be important to have the support of a program director, dean, as well as a provost or other administrator. Although their support is important, it is critical that the research team not allow the institutions (which tend to have interests antithetical to those of the critical-emancipatory tradition) to co-opt their social change agendas. Indeed, such research can be "sexy" from a public relations perspective, as many universities have global agendas in the developing world. It is important that such PR not exploit a more vulnerable project partner, or damage the integrity of the researcher.

Even though funding, institutional support, facilities, and other resources are certainly vital components of critical-emancipatory PAR, the most important resource is the PAR researcher himself or herself. In the context of working in a disaster in the Global South, many obstacles abound. The context and concomitant infrastructure deprivations create problems related to devastation of already fragile infrastructure, technological limitations, and communication and translation problems. Thus, Kindon, Pain, and Kesby (2007) have argued that PAR researchers should have some of the following assets or characteristics to facilitate the PAR process in such challenging environments:

> hybrids of scholar/activist where neither is privileged; mavericks/heretics; patient; sociable and collaborative; able to be flexible and accommodate chaos, uncertainty and messiness; able to tolerate paradoxes and puzzles and sense their beauty and humour; attracted to complex, multi-dimensional, intractable, dynamic problems that can only be partially resolved; engaged in embodied and emotional intellectual practice. (p. 14)

This last characteristic is one that is especially relevant in a postdisaster setting.

The first trip of Pyles (one of the authors of this chapter) to Haiti as a PAR researcher in February 2010, about 5 weeks after a catastrophic earthquake devastated the country, serves as an important reminder. Pyles was taken to a mass grave that was said to have some 60,000 bodies buried there. This was indeed an "embodied and emotional" experience. It had a palpable feel, smell, and emotional flavor to it. Being willing to be present for such experiences and reflect on them in relation to the goals of the project is a critical asset.

APPLICATIONS IN THE GLOBAL SOUTH AND OTHER MARGINALIZED LOCATIONS

Chambers and Guijt (2011) have argued that PAR methods such as participatory mapping, matrices, well-being ranking, and causal and linking diagramming are more advantageous and better suited for inquiry purposes in the developing world. This is because they are visual (rather than verbal), collective (rather than individual), and compare (rather than measure) (Chambers & Guijt, 2011). PAR in the Global South draws on indigenous voices, beliefs, and practices; collective narratives and actions (Lykes, 2013); social diversity and local knowledge as the basis of solutions (Chambers & Guijt, 2011); and people's struggles as motives for change (Symes & Jasser, 2011).

The uses of PAR in the Global South are diverse and creative in their applications. For example, Chambers and Guijt (2011) suggested that participatory rural appraisal, as one of the applications of PAR, has been widely utilized in a range of development domains, such as watershed development, social forestry, women's programs, health programs, water and sanitation, emergency programs, and many others. Extending beyond the "research" element of PAR, the examples of "participatory" "action" in the Global South abound. Such participatory methodologies are exemplified through cooperative inquiry, community exchanges, citizen juries, participatory videos, and theater for development (Cornwall, 2011). In the case study that follows, we present an application of critical-emancipatory PAR in postearthquake Haiti.

LORETTA PYLES'S PARTICIPATORY ACTION RESEARCH IN HAITI AFTER THE 2010 EARTHQUAKE

When a devastating earthquake hit Port-au-Prince, Haiti, and its environs in January 2010, I became intensely interested in the impact, relief efforts, and the media discourse around it. Drawing on my knowledge and experiences of watching disaster capitalism in action in post-Katrina New Orleans, I began to critically inquire into the social production of the relief process. Right after the tremor had shaken Haiti, elites gave priority to immediate emergency action over long-term recovery planning. Although understandable, such an approach is problematic as it overlooks the complexity of needs and sustainable recovery in the long term. To conduct relief and recovery work effectively and sustainably requires deeper understanding of the histories, recovery needs, and visions identified by the affected communities.

Serendipitously, I met a community organizer visiting my university from Haiti who was looking for partners to advance recovery efforts in rural Haiti. He was specifically looking for someone to initiate an action research study focused on the capacities of rural communities to engage in development and recovery work. As a scholar-activist and feminist practitioner, I knew that this study had to be participatory, and I advocated for such an approach. The PAR approach turned out to resonate with the local actors who would become involved in the project, actualizing an unarticulated intention of the group to advance their own capabilities and to be more in charge of the assessments that had been done "on" them in the past. Indeed, the actors all had experiences with NGOs coming into their communities, conducting an assessment, and then either (1) providing the kinds of services that the NGO intended to provide before the assessment anyway or (2) disappearing altogether and engaging in no actions.

The details of this project have been articulated and analyzed in other venues (Pyles, Rodrigue & André, 2011; Svistova, Pyles, & André, in press; Pyles, under review;), focusing on some of the postcolonialist complexities such as how challenging it was to include, let alone center, women in the research process. Our purpose here, though, is to provide an example of the complex phases of a PAR research project in the Global South, as a way to clarify the model that we have presented here. The major objective of this research in Haiti was to learn about the impact of the earthquake and visions of recovery for rural grass-roots organizations in 11 communities. Through such a process, local actors were invited to Port-au-Prince and trained to engage in PAR, so that they could go back home and learn about the experiences of other organizations and actors in their own communities. This way, local people had an opportunity to articulate their own needs and ideas of interventions, eventually inviting outsiders willing to honor their visions to participate as funders and partners, in effect turning the development and humanitarian aid model on its head.

The *context* of rural Haiti is saturated by postcolonial development practices. In addition, ongoing development problems and the earthquake itself had a negative impact on our capabilities (e.g., emotional, technological) to accomplish the research. Thus, context has a juicy saliency throughout the phases of the process, and it dictated the *research* itself, including the methods used, the questions asked, the importance of local actors' collecting the data, and the ongoing reflection and analysis of the data.

Action/transformation was perhaps the most important component in working in postearthquake Haiti, where there are indeed so many community members living in misery and in need of real-time results. Besides the enhanced critical awareness and capabilities of the researchers, genuine changes in the environment were not quickly forthcoming, as the research process was underresourced and slow to unfold. In fact, it was not until four years later that I learned that the project resulted in the purchasing of land for a new children's school in one of the case study communities.

Because of historical marginalization and hegemonic foreign-local actor relations, *participation* became a moment-to-moment practice of sharing power, engaging in dialogue, and building capacity. What is noteworthy and relevant for this type of PAR in addressing a wicked problem is that so much of the process is collaborative; thus, relationship-building, as a function of participation, plays a central role in all phases of the research and action phases.

Figure 5.2 details the multiple phases of the project from conception through evaluation/reflection. The table is presented in a linear style, but it was anything but a linear process; indeed, it was an iterative process that required flexibility, spontaneity, and self-reflexivity. For this process to truly be decolonizing, each phase must be interrogated, and there must be constant critical analysis, self-inquiry, and group learning. Thus, the four cornerstones of critical-emancipatory PAR in the Global South, articulated in Figure 5.1—context, research, action/transformation, and participation—are all reflected across and within the phases of this project.

Project Phases
1. Pre-planning and project development
2. Workshop on PAR with delegates/lead interviewers in Port-Au-Prince
3. Delegate mentoring with assistant interviewers
4. Interview team conducts qualitative interviews with organizational leaders in communities
5. Delegates report back in Port-au-Prince and reflect
6. Transcribe and translate data
7. Analyze data
8. Workshop with delegates and communities on project management and other topics
9. Present and publish preliminary analysis and community needs
10. Establish MOUs with funders for new projects that emerge from findings
11. Implement projects
12. Reflect on and evaluate process and projects

Figure 5.2 PAR Phases in Postdisaster Haiti from Pre-Project Planning through Reflection and Evaluation.

CONCLUSION

In our understanding and articulation of critical-emancipatory PAR, we have brought attention to the issues oftentimes disregarded by the mainstream output-input-oriented, impersonal, control-driven, and value-free scientific practice of the Global North. We have suggested throughout the chapter that such cold practices of the North serve to widen and strengthen the gap between the Global North and the Global South in search of objective truth and in service to rational-technical interventions to complex, wicked social problems, such as disasters. We have presented critical-emancipatory PAR as an antidote that, perhaps paradoxically to some social scientists, positions scientific practice as a subjective, morally, and ethically charged service wherein the research process is informed and guided by identity development, values, emotions, relationships, histories of oppression, and new visions of reality.

To this end, we have pleaded to the reader the importance of remembering the past and creating change, interaction by interaction, practice by practice, and day by day in the present in order to transform the future. As transnational borders are widely open, our responsibility as the makers of the history with embodied privilege is to act today, in ways that build global bridges, not fortresses, for the just and loving future. For even if it is through a small, largely unnoticed act of participatory action research, someone's world changes. We researchers also change.

6

Summary Reflections and Lessons Learned

Hal A. Lawson, Christine T. Bozlak, James C. Caringi,
Loretta Pyles, and Janine M. Jurkowski

INTRODUCTION

Participatory action research (PAR) is a special methodology structured to develop new knowledge and articulate theory as two or more investigators strive to solve practical problems in real-world contexts. Significantly, these investigators include practicing professionals and laypersons from all walks of life who have expertise about these problems and whose participation is essential to both problem-solving and knowledge generation. PAR gives expression to Kurt Lewin's (1951) claim: One of the best ways to gain knowledge and understanding about any phenomenon is by trying to change it in its naturally occurring contexts.

As the preceding chapters have demonstrated, PAR uniquely is founded on five additional claims. These claims differentiate PAR from a variety of action research methodologies and also from intervention research.

- Local stakeholders from diverse walks of life (e.g., social work practitioners, adolescents, older adults, politicians, parents and grandparents, vulnerable immigrants, children in foster care) have strengths, starting with their invaluable expertise about the problem(s) needing to be understood, investigated, and addressed.

- One of the best ways to gain knowledge and understanding about any phenomenon is by preparing these local stakeholders to be co-researchers and then engaging them in PAR's integrated research, theory development, and problem-solving process.

- PAR's steady progression toward more equitable relationships between academic researchers and local stakeholders desirably reflects and strengthens the ideals for relationships in democratic societies, especially the contributions of these relationships to individual, group, organizational, and societal learning.

- Insofar as PAR's investigative team is representative of local diversity, it provides quality assurance safeguards for culturally competent problem-solving, knowledge generation, and theory articulation.

- When complex, adaptive and wicked problems need to be clarified, understood, and addressed, and "one and done studies" will not suffice, PAR merits consideration as a research option, alone or in combination with other methods.

These claims unite the several chapters in this book and also showcase their respective and collective contributions. Framed by these claims, PAR can be viewed as a special social practice.

PRACTICE COMPETENCIES AS RESEARCH COMPETENCIES WITH ETHICAL IMPERATIVES

When PAR is framed and offered as a special social practice, it can be aligned and connected with several defining features of social work practice as well as with identical practices in sister fields such as public health, community psychology, and education. For example, social work practice ideally is strengths-based, solution-focused, and culturally competent, and so is PAR. Oftentimes, social work practice involves group work, and PAR depends on it. Multidimensional social work practice prioritizes micro-, meso-, and macrolevels for every person-in-environment need or problem, and so does PAR. Increasingly, social work practice and policy directed at complex adaptive needs and wicked problems necessitates both interprofessional and community collaboration, and so does PAR.

Such profound correspondence between practice frameworks/competencies and PAR frameworks/competencies is not contrived. PAR is indeed a particular kind of social practice, one that is iterative and recursive. PAR accomplishes "social work" precisely because it engages teams of investigators in the all-important work known as the social construction of reality (Berger & Luckmann, 1967).

What's more, PAR is a critical social work practice insofar as it is launched by a profound question: *What and whose knowledge matters most when urgent needs, problems, and opportunities must be addressed?*

As the preceding chapters with their respective examples indicate, PAR provides a unique answer to this question. Because PAR engages everyday people from diverse walks of life, it protects researchers in every field from provincial, self-serving, arrogant, and potentially harmful knowledge claims—and with an important reminder. In human services professions, all such knowledge claims are designed to be "actionable," which means that they are expected to guide and inform the development of recommended practices and policies, especially ones called empirically based and research supported. PAR, suitably designed and conducted in accordance with its regulative and constitutive rules, contributes to and expands conceptions of "empirically based and research-supported" policies and practices.

In the same vein, *PAR is enlightening* when it illuminates problems, needs, and opportunities in new ways. *It is consequential* when it makes a difference in how these problems, needs, and opportunities are framed, named, and addressed. In turn, *PAR is useful* when its actionable knowledge has instrumental value when something must be done.

PAR thus offers distinctive advantages. At the same time, PAR is selective and limited. The preceding chapters have justified these twin claims, together with two important cautions.

TWO CAUTIONS

The first caution also is a reminder from the introduction and chapter 1. PAR is not a panacea. It is fit for some purposes, but not others. More fundamentally, if the researcher is not prepared to accept its regulative and constitutive rules and strive to implement them with fidelity, PAR should not be adopted and attempted. More boldly, PAR done badly not only exacerbates problems; it also creates new ones—needlessly.

The second caution: Despite misguided views that PAR lacks rigor and provides the easy way to research and practice, it is not easy to design, implement, and complete. To the contrary, in many ways PAR is more challenging than conventional research. These challenges are especially apparent when PAR is combined with conventional qualitative and quantitative methods with interdisciplinary research teams. Challenges also arise when everyday people (community members, practitioners, policy leaders), especially the most vulnerable ones, must be recruited, prepared, and engaged in PAR initiatives that last a long time. This last descriptor, "last a long time," emphasizes PAR sustainability with its own set of challenges. All in all, PAR's inherent complexity and design difficulties must be evaluated before commitments are made to it.

This caution is especially relevant to master's theses and doctoral dissertations. Although several articles and a useful book offer direction and guidance (Herr & Anderson, 2015; Herr, 2014; Nygreen, 2009/2010), unforeseen challenges and obstacles are the norm, not the exception. Arguably, no student should undertake a PAR thesis or dissertation without a chair with PAR expertise and experience. This caution also can be viewed as a lesson learned, paving the way for several others that follow.

KEY PAR LESSONS LEARNED

Aiming to facilitate other researchers' efficient, effective, and faithful implementation of PAR, the authors collaborated to generate practical, consequential lessons learned. Our reflections were guided by the following, generative question: Think back to when you first began your PAR research. If you knew then what you know now, what would you do differently, and better? Why?

The following lessons learned thus are collective products. They are not rank ordered. Significantly, these reflective lessons learned are not mainstays in PAR generic textbooks and advocacy briefs, especially ones that present an overly rosy picture and leave readers with the impression that PAR is really easy to implement and complete. Our lessons learned suggest otherwise.

We have settled on a developmental progression for these lessons learned. They begin with graduate students, especially doctoral students. Later, the focus expands to early career researchers and others interested in adding PAR to their repertoires.

Together these lessons learned are offered as time-saving and resource-maximizing challenges. Although they might be viewed as cautions and even warnings that discourage PAR, in fact they are facilitators for successful and efficient PAR designs.

Special Lessons for Graduate Students

Cease viewing research and practice as separate and at times competing priorities undertaken by very different people. When some of us began ourdoctoral programs, we were under the impression that research was an entirely separate endeavor from all other social work interventions and activities. In fact, that is what we were taught by professors and other experts.

Our first lesson learned is that research and practice need to happen at the same time because together they have more traction. This is especially the case when both research and practice are framed as adaptive learning and problem-solving for complex needs and problems. Integrated, flexible research and practice strategies are especially salient to continuing efforts to advance social and economic justice for vulnerable, marginalized, and oppressed people.

Do not underestimate the challenges associated with a PAR dissertation or master's thesis. Students aspiring to conduct PAR dissertations and theses are one of the primary audiences for this book. We applaud this ambition and offer our unyielding support. We also hope that by reading this book you are aware of the commitment and sacrifices that are necessary in order to complete a PAR project. It is not easy as a student to commit to the time needed to establish trusting relationships with community partners. Remember: This process that can take years before any data are collected because participants need the time, preparation, and supports to learn how to work together and co-design the study. Even when this consensus has been developed and co-investigators have been prepared, the institutional review board (IRB) process remains, and it is followed by data collection, analysis and interpretation, and joint dissemination of the findings.

One of the authors found it mentally challenging to do this while watching members of her doctoral program cohort complete their more traditional dissertations and graduate much more expeditiously to the next stages of their life and career. In brief, if you make the choice to pursue a PAR project as a dissertation, we recommend that you take the time to create a network of other like-minded students and faculty, outside your dissertation committee and potentially outside your university. You will need their support and inspiration.

Be prepared to unlearn everything you thought you knew. As a researcher just embarking on PAR projects, it can be surprising and confusing to find yourself in a situation where you are simultaneously being trained to demonstrate expertise as a "scholar" in the academic setting, while at the same time needing to strip yourself of this expertise when working with community partners. Put simply, it can often feel like an identity crisis to beginning PAR researchers. We often hear about the benefits of higher education, especially during the educational setting, and we become convinced that education propels people to power and superiority. For the student or beginning researcher who would like to pursue PAR projects, it is challenging to know that you are no longer the sole expert; and also that you need to be on equal footing with community partners.

It is especially challenging when you discover that you must relearn everything you thought you knew about a phenomenon, gaining enlightenment from people who may not be respected due to their place in society, either because of age, education, socioeconomic standing, or other factors. The best advice we can give is to understand and accept two privileges you enjoy. One is that you are coming from a place of privilege, starting with your advanced education and including the quality of your life. The other is the privilege PAR provides you—namely, a new self-understanding and sense of humility that you did not learn every-thing there was to learn within the university walls. With PAR you will come to realize that (a) there is so much more than meets the eye in realworld situations; (b) gaps in your formal education and experience contribute to your ignorance; (c) you come from a position of privilege and constantly must guard against the biases this privilege brings; and (d) everyday people are some of your best teachers. PAR investigators learn all of this and more, and their learning and professional develop-ment via PAR helps to account for their preferences for it.

Academic and Community Social Life Worlds

PAR is a social construction created by academic researchers. Although PAR has some roots in community-based practice, its origins and home base ultimately lie within the academy. Institutionalized academia necessitates that PAR be a delimited endeavor with specific parameters, including a clear beginning, middle, and end. In contrast, leaders of nonprofit organizations and grass-roots actors do not view the work in this way, even though they value the relationships, the capacity-building, and the action orientations that PAR offers.

In fact, the work of local actors is so fluid that grasping what PAR is and accomplishes can be elusive. Under these conditions, the essence of PAR becomes a kind of moving target, shifting from moment to moment—from community education to community-building to orga-nizing to advocacy. Thus, it is important that a PAR social work practitio-ner not become too attached to PAR and the strict boundaries researchers are inclined to draw around it. This may imply that social work scholars need to frame the work that they are doing in different ways to differ-ent actors—in a manner akin to language translators and interpreters. For example, for one audience—the IRB—PAR is formal research. At the same time, it is viewed as one phase of a community-organizing cam-paign among local actors. At the end of the day, PAR is a fluid social prac-tice. It necessitates embracing serendipity, diversity, and flux.

A Bicultural Research Identity and Orientation

PAR practitioners are bicultural people engaged in social praxis par excel-lence. PAR offers practitioners the opportunity to operate in a kind of liminal space contoured by university and community boundaries. Engaged PAR social work scholars work at the intersection of these boundaries, sometimes bridging them and at other times challenged by their parameters and requirements. There is no escape from the tensions and uncertainties.

It is normal for us to feel like we do not quite belong in either world. At the same time, we are forced to operate biculturally, adopting both the norms of academic culture and the norms of community practice. Oftentimes, our academic colleagues will not fully understand us. At the same time, local community actors always will view us as outsiders at some level.

Rather than bemoan these situations, we can realize that life and work at and inside university-community boundaries offers a powerful place for our work. For example, engaging in PAR provides us with an insider perspective within the community, one that helps us to actualize more community-engaged universities. It also puts us in a position to analyze social work practices and advance social theory in a way that ivory tower scholars and social work practitioners are not in a position to do. Thus, we find ourselves on a threshold, with a foot in each world. All the while, we are engaged in praxis, striving to move the social work and its sister professions ever forward in the shared quest to address the vulnerabilities created by oppressive social and economic injustice.

University Researchers Need a Local Cultural Broker

When community-based PAR is undertaken, it is important to have a person representing the project on the ground in the community, one who engages community partners regularly. Professors must worry about teaching and other university-based activities and thus are constrained in how much "face time" they are able to provide to community-based PAR team members. A local community representative who serves as a cultural broker is especially important for working with vulnerable populations who may require extra effort to build trust and project commitment. In the case of Communities for Healthy Living (CHL; chapter 4), this cultural broker was stationed at the organization where low-income families spent time. Consequently, he always was accessible for quick questions or comments, informal conversations, and engaging parents outside the meeting in project activities. Also, by being in the community organization, he was able to learn organizational policies and processes that affected parents and the research project. As a result, he was able to navigate the organization and embed the CHL project within the organization.

Authentic, not Token, Participation

It is essential to honor and promote the truly participatory-democratic nature of PAR. It is all too easy to fall into the trap of minimally including practicing professionals and community members due to the pressures of time, funder requirements, and wanting to get things accomplished efficiently, especially so when academic researchers must balance competing priorities, including teaching, advising, and publication requirements. Under these circumstances, time-saving PAR shortcuts may be alluring. Reduced participation by practicing professionals and community members is one such shortcut.

All such shortcuts, but especially participation, need to be prevented and avoided. Participation is not only essential for social justice but also for effective outcomes that have traction and sustainability in organizations. "Experts" include those who are participants in the systems we want to learn about.

Back to basics: PAR requires an intense dedication to stakeholder inclusion in the research process, starting from the first moments of formulating a research question. PAR requires joining with partners in their organizations and communities. In other words, we need to go to them—in places and settings they choose. Quite simply, it is difficult to be participatory and complete PAR if we do not show up.

An Infrastructure for Community-Based Participatory Action Research

It is important to have an infrastructure for community-based projects involving formal university-community partnerships, but especially ones that address complex and adaptive social, economic, political, and health issues. The main reason: The community-based PAR project itself becomes increasingly complex, so much so that it can be an adaptive problem.

The university-community infrastructure needs to prioritize resource generation and allocation, especially money, time, and supports. For example, if the budget allows for funding to compensate the organization for use of its space and its person time, the leadership should make it happen.

In the same vein, structural accommodations, and if possible, financial rewards for lay community members are very important PAR facilitators. After all, low-income people often receive messages from professionals that professional schedules and priorities matter most. This sends an unfortunate metamessage about the superior power and authority of the professional, one that ultimately erodes and prevents genuinely democratic relationships among university researchers and other people serving on the PAR team.

Especially when low-income families with children are involved in PAR, their scheduling needs and ecological realities must be prioritized. For example, PAR and community advisory board meetings may need to be held in the evening, and child care will need to be provided. In the case of CHL in chapter 4, dinners were provided for parents and children alike. This simple, important gesture facilitated their engagement and also helped to build solid working relationships among university researchers, community professionals, and parents.

Time Is a Precious Resource

Double the amount of time you have allocated for the PAR design and implementation and then consider contingency plans for allocating yet more time for your scheduled research to be completed. This lesson learned can be introduced by analogy. PAR design and implementation is akin to organizing and mobilizing diverse people from a variety of places for focused, strategic collective action. A simple rule is as follows: The greater the complexity of the research problem, the greater the diversity and size of the PAR participants; and the greater the political resistance to the PAR initiative overall, the longer it will take to successfully mount and complete the PAR investigation. For doctoral students needing to finish their dissertations and early career faculty members who are worried about a tenure and promotion clock, this lesson learned has special salience.

In the same vein, the faculty researcher needs to make time in his or her schedule to conduct this type of research. In fact, the researcher may need to work with department chairs, directors, and deans to obtain released time from some obligations as well as to gain project adminis-tration assistance from support staff.

In exchange for more time for PAR and community-based participa-tory research (CBPR), the researcher offers the host department, school, college, and university the political capital gained from high-visibility projects conducted in local communities. For public colleges and uni-versities that depend on politicians' perceptions of their institution's contributions to the problems of the day, this political capital is a valuable resource and an incentive for granting released time for PAR researchers and providing administrative supports.

Endemic Tensions and Dilemmas

Anticipate, plan for, and do not get sidetracked by endemic dilemmas in some PAR investigations. Nygreen (2009–2010) provided a compelling account of several important dilemmas, including the ones she did not anticipate and how they impacted her and her research. For example, she proceeded with a critical feminist perspective with the aim of chal-lenging and changing the unequal, unjust relationships of the domi-nant social order. She found that her project had the opposite effect. Ironically, at times her work reproduced these relationships. Although Nygreen's account of her encounter with this dilemma and others is not exhaustive, it provides an important PAR planning and implementation platform for all PAR investigators, but especially doctoral students and early career investigators.

Certainly, it is important to take stock of these dilemmas and make all relevant preparations. However, all dilemmas, together with PAR tensions and ambiguities, need to be placed in proper perspective. All manner of research methodologies have their own tensions, ambigui-ties, and even dilemmas. Thus, every researcher confronts these chal-lenges. Because there is no escape from them in one form or another, these challenges should not rule out PAR. The priority is to be prepared so that they can be prevented whenever possible.

Conflict and Resistance

Anticipate and plan for conflict and resistance, and have prevention and early intervention strategies ready. This PAR lesson can be viewed as a corollary of Murphy's law—if something can go wrong, it will. A brief explanation follows.

Conflict is endemic in all human collaborations, and some of it can be a powerful stimulus for creative thinking, planning, and knowledge generation. The key is to make it manageable and even productive by keeping the PAR climate positive and respectful. Formal norms, rules, and operational protocols (e.g., chapter 2) are both PAR process facilitators and preventive measures for negative and destructive conflict. In the same vein, PAR depends fundamentally on the establishment of conducive social settings (Seidman, 2012).

Resistance is inevitable when total consensus among all PAR participants has not and cannot be achieved. Under these circumstances, the PAR investigator must strike a delicate balance. The research needs to proceed in lieu of being halted by one or two participants at the same time that efforts continue to gain buy-in. These efforts oftentimes include the explicit pledge to be on the lookout for the naysayers' perceptions of needs, problems, constraints, and barriers. Overall, a combination of individual needs and group dynamics is implicated here, and clinical skills for both individual and group practice come in handy.

One preventive strategy is to strive to achieve the best mix of the right people, ensuring diverse representation and participation, but also prioritizing people who have worked together previously. Another is to avoid favoritism and special privileges granted to some participants. In all such cases, a researcher's clinical skills come in handy.

Aiming for Cause-and-Effect Logic

Strive to help PAR participants appreciate causal logic by employing PAR tools that make this logic visual and richly experiential. Community members (aka laypersons), and especially the most vulnerable ones, are critically important PAR co-investigators. They have the potential for causal reasoning and intervention logic, but in many instances no one has prepared them for it. PAR offers this opportunity. Simple, practical logic models provide one visual tool for participants to learn causal logic, making it action oriented (chapter 2 provides an example, including the example of PAR participants who taught others in their agencies to develop logic models.)

Kurt Lewin's (1951) framework for force field analysis is a companion strategy. Essentially, participants co-construct a two-column framework with matched pairs of priorities. One column provides the forces, factors, and actors that are conducive to change, and the companion column identifies the forces, factors, and actors that constrain, resist, and prohibit change. The main idea is compelling: PAR often must build on the facilitators and, at the same time, address the constraints, obstacles, and barriers. PAR participants learn causal logic as they provide this conceptual mapping. And later, they can be applauded for their contributions to theory—because this is what conceptual mapping enables.

PARTICIPATORY ACTION RESEARCH AND INSTITUTIONAL REVIEW BOARDS

One of the main goals of the IRB is to protect human subjects in biomedical and behavioral research. The review process consists of risk-benefit analysis to determine whether research should be conducted. Because of PAR's unique aims, structures, and rules, issues may arise in the process of gaining approval from IRBs to conduct the research. This situation is especially likely when IRB members lack formal PAR preparation, expertise, and experience.

Issues that may concern IRBs start with core, defining aspects of PAR that are integral to the methodology. Examples include access to data about study participants, lack of long-term, clearly defined timelines, and a research model that includes nonscientists serving as investigators (Blumenthal, 2006; Brown et al., 2010). Delays in receiving approval for research are normal, and they can have wide-ranging consequences for researchers and their PAR co-investigators.

Several IRB strategies are designed to ensure that the IRB review procedure is quick, informed, and positive. For example, the materials for application should be prepared long before the anticipated start date for the research project in case the review process takes longer than expected, or requires materials to be resubmitted after alterations. In the same light, the pocess of preparing materials for IRB review requires forethought regarding what the IRB is expecting to see and how the investigator can make the review process easier for them (Gelmon, Malone, & Yancey,, 2007).

Some universities have sample proposals that can be requested from the IRB or accessed digitally to help guide preparation. These samples are important tools to help match a proposal to that specific IRB's expectations (Gelmon et al., 2007). In addition, universities often have staff working for the IRB who are willing to answer questions regarding proposals and potential stumbling blocks in the IRB process for the particular research proposal (Gelmon et al., 2007). One of the authors of this book (Bozlak) took this step prior to beginning her dissertation research. Consulting with IRB staff also has the benefit of allowing the researcher to get an idea of the types of research the IRB is most familiar reviewing.

Due to the differences in language used by PAR researchers (versus more traditional human subjects research), it is important that investigators clearly define all the terminology that is used in their proposal, be it in-text or in a glossary. This special effort, in addition to a coherent and well-substantiated description of the proposal, will allow IRB reviewers to familiarize themselves with the terms used in PAR, enabling them to offer a more informed review. It is also useful to list any prospective changes that may occur over the course of the research, changes prompted by input from PAR co-researchers, so that the IRB can better understand how and in what way participants' input will be handled in the context of research (Ahmed et al., 2007). Although it is impossible to predict what input will be received from the PAR co-investigators and what course of action will be taken, it is useful for the IRB to see examples of how this process could actually work.

Although an investigator can take several steps such as these to increase the chances of receiving IRB approval, in some cases additional institutional action needs to take place. For instance, some investigators find that their IRBs are open to holding educational sessions to educate and inform IRB members of the methodologies and practice of PAR to allow them to better evaluate these types of projects (Brydon-Miller & Greenwood, 2006). Others suggest that PAR researchers should encourage their colleagues who also conduct PAR to serve on IRBs in order to provide an informed voice in review decisions.

Experts also propose that IRB-PAR liaisons be utilized. The liaisons would approve or disapprove of changes in PAR stemming from community input (Brydon-Miller &Greenwood, 2006). These broader actions, though not necessary to one's own IRB review process, allow for a more educated and streamlined review process at research institutions.

Researchers should anticipate additional challenges in conducting PAR, especially if the research participants and collaborators are considered vulnerable subgroups of the population, such as youth. For example, in the case of international research in the Global South, Pyles faced significant challenges when trying to communicate to the IRB the logistics of employing local Haitian actors to be co-researchers.

In the same vein, Bozlak and Kelley (chapter 3) detailed the challenges to conducting youth participatory action research (YPAR). The IRB process was a significant challenge for one of the case studies they presented. In this particular case, the principal investigator (Bozlak) took extra steps to ensure a smooth institutional review process, such as meeting with staff associated with her IRB and communicating with other researchers who had conducted YPAR studies. Unfortunately, these actions did not prevent the study from requiring several additional months of review by the fully convened IRB. The review process resulted in an approved research protocol. However, many of the PAR-related elements of the original research proposal were weakened by the IRB.

The IRB is not the only potential institutional hurdle for PAR researchers to overcome. For example, dissertation committees and reviewers for internal research grants may also offer challenges to the aspiring PAR researcher. One of the authors (Bozlak) was required by her dissertation committee to conduct a pilot study with a group of youth prior to being given permission to proceed with her proposed YPAR dissertation study. The purpose of the pilot study was to demonstrate to the committee that youth, in this case young adolescents, would have enough to say and contribute on the phenomenon of interest. This pilot study prolonged the duration of the study and the dissertation process because it required all the elements of the primary research (i.e., collaboration with community partners, study design, IRB approval, recruitment and parental consent, and data collection and analysis). It is possible that if there were more examples in the literature of youth engagement in PAR studies that resulted in advocacy, this pilot study would not have been a requirement for the dissertation.

We are hopeful that the emphasis on community-engaged research and community-based PAR by the federal government and other funders (e.g., charitable foundations, state governmental agencies) is reeducating the academic community on what constitutes scholarly research. We also are hopeful that those with institutional oversight of this research are modifying their practices accordingly. However, these responses cannot be assumed. Just as lead PAR investigations must educate participants in community settings, these same researchers must be prepared to educate their colleagues and advocate for PAR in the home university. In short, universities also are sites for responsive and proactive social change, in this case in IRB members' views of, and safeguards for, research, together with all-important human subject protections and quality assurance safeguards.

CONCLUSION

PAR clearly is fraught with challenges. The challenges include getting research approved by the IRB, sustaining relationships with local actors, navigating the endemic tensions of disparate social locations of co-researchers, and striving to persuade skeptical faculty members about the merits of PAR. The preceding chapters have identified and described these several challenges, while emphasizing PAR's importance and relevance for particular kinds of needs, problems, and opportunities.

Notwithstanding challenges, PAR is an important, potent, and unique methodology, and it is ripe with important opportunities. It is gratifying to design and complete. It has the potential to be a life-changing experience for academic researchers and community participants alike.

In contrast to the PAR pioneers who proceeded without clear, coherent theoretical frameworks and field-tested methodologies, succeeding generations of PAR investigators have an array of alternatives. Risking the exclusion of key PAR pioneers, and borrowing a phrase from sociologist Robert Merton, all of us can stand on the shoulders of PAR giants, including Freire, Lewin, Stringer, Greenwood, and Levin. In fact, our lessons learned, especially those offered in this last chapter, can be traced back to these PAR pioneers' theories, methodological alternatives, and lessons learned.

Mirroring what these pioneers learned, our insights in this book derive from our direct experiences. In contrast to "research experts as removed observers"—in fact, distanced spectators—we authors have been directly, intimately, and intensely engaged in the all-important work of building democratic relationships with community members to generate knowledge that contributes to the development of a more just and sustainable world. Like the giants on whose shoulders we stand, PAR defines who we are in addition to the important work we do.

Key Websites for Participatory Action Research

GETTING STARTED

AR+ Action Research (An International Resource)
http://actionresearchplus.com/
Caledonia University (Scotland): 16 PAR tenets
http://www.caledonia.org.uk/par.htm
Center for Integrating Research Action
http://www.cira-unc.org
Chevalier and Buckles (2013): PAR Tools and Resources
http://www.participatoryactionresearch.net/
Community-Campus Partnership for Health
https://ccph.memberclicks.net/
Community Tool Box
http://ctb.ku.edu/
Infed.org on Action Research and Its Variations
http://infed.org/mobi/action-research/
The Public Science Project
http://publicscienceproject.org/
Wikipedia
http://www.ask.com/wiki/Participatory_action_research?o=2801&qsrc=999&
    ad=doubleDown&an=apn&ap=ask.com

EXAMPLES OF UNIVERSITY CENTERS FOR ACTION RESEARCH AND PAR

Cornell University (New York) Participatory Action Research Network
http://www.cparn.org/p/par-resources-and-literature.html
Center for Collaborative Action Research, Pepperdine University (California).
http://cadres.pepperdine.edu/ccar/define.html
Durham University, UK. PAR Toolkit (R. Pain, G. Whitman, & D. Milledge &
   Lune Rivers Trust)
https://www.dur.ac.uk/resources/beacon/PARtoolkit.pdf
Sonoma State University (California) Center for Community Engagement:
   Differences Among Various Kinds of Action Research
http://www.sonoma.edu/cce/faculty/differences_cbr_cbpr_ar.html
University of Strathclyde, UK
http://www.strath.ac.uk/aer/materials/2designstrategiesineducationalresea
   rch/unit3/participatoryactionresearch/

VIDEO RESOURCES

Dr. E. Alana James (Walden University): Complex, Adaptive Issues and the
   Uses of PAR to Solve Them
http://www.youtube.com/watch?v=s-SAJPF5xiA
Professor Abe Oudshoorn (University of Western Ontario) on PAR in his work
   with homeless youths
http://www.youtube.com/watch?v=yrF7cVESMzg
Professor Michelle Fine on Youth Participatory Action Research
http://www.youtube.com/watch?v=vuXoKKXp6QM
Dr. William Oswald on Community-Based, Participatory Action Research
http://www.youtube.com/watch?v=Ehy002Kep0k
Introduction to Video Methods With PAR
http://www.youtube.com/watch?v=o3xsttz8F8o
PAR in Chicago Public Schools: An Example Project http://www.youtube.com/
   watch?v=L25zCvH5y10
Dr. E. Alana James (Walden University): Tips and Tools for Writing Action
   Research Papers and Dissertations. (See also her new book from Sage
   Publications, *Dissertation Writing Made Easier and Faster.*)
http://www.youtube.com/watch?v=ybyErm7zABI

CRITICAL PAR AND INTERNATIONAL DEVELOPMENT

PAR in Bolivia (in Spanish with subtitles) http://www.youtube.com/watch?v=
    lNSl4GMedk8
Participatory Action Research for Sustainable Community Development
http://postgrowth.org/participatory-action-research-
par-for-sustainable-community-development/
Participatory Research for Sustainable Livelihoods
http://www.iisd.org/casl/caslguide/par.htm
Pedagogy and Theatre of the Oppressed
http://www.ptoweb.org
The Praxis Project
http://thepraxisproject.org

References

Abbott, A. (2001). *Chaos of disciplines*. Chicago: University of Chicago Press.

ACT for Youth. (n.d.) *Positive youth development resource manual*. Retrieved from: http://ecommons.cornell.edu/bitstream/1813/21946/2/PYD_Resource Manual.pdf

Adkins, S., Sherwood, N. E., Story, M., & Davis, M. (2004). Physical activity among African American girls: the role of parents and the home environment. *Obesity Research, 12 Suppl*, 38S–45S. DOI: 10.1038/oby.2004.267

Ahmed, S., Beversdorf, S., Flicker, S., Travers, R., & Shore, N. CCPH/Bioethics Center Educational Conference Call Series on IRBs and Ethical Issues in Research: Call 6. "IRB Reform: Changing Policy and Practice to Protect Communities". June 25, 2007.

Allen-Scott, L. K., Hatfield, J. M., & McIntyre, L. (2014). A scoping review of unintended harm associated with public health interventions: Towards a typology and an understanding of underlying factors. *International Journal of Public Health, 59*(1), 1–12.

Allina-Pisano, E. (2009). Imperialism and the colonial experience. In Haslam, P.A., Schafer, J. and Beaudet, P. (Eds), *Introduction to international development: Approaches, actors and issues*. Don Mills, ON: Oxford University Press.

Amsden, J., & Van Wynsberghe, R. (2005). Community mapping as a research tool with youth. *Action Research, 3*(4), 353–377.

Anda, R.F., Butchart, A., Felitti, V., & Brown, D. (2010). Building a framework of global surveillance of the public health implications of adverse childhood experiences. *American Journal of Preventive Medicine, 39*(1), 93–98.

Anderson, S., & Whitaker, R. (2009). Prevalence of obesity among US preschool children in different racial and ethnic groups. *Archives of Pediatrics and Adolescent Medicine, 163*(4), 344–348.

Andrews, K. R., Silk, K. S., & Eneli, I. U. (2010). Parents as health promoters: A theory of planned behavior perspective on the prevention of childhood obesity. *J Health Commun, 15*(1), 95–107. DOI: 10.1080/10810730903460567

Anderson-Butcher, D., Lawson, H., & Barkdull, C. (2003). An evaluation of child welfare design teams in four states. *Journal of Health and Social Policy,* 15(3–4), 131–161.

Argyris, C. (2004). *Reasons and rationalizations: The limits to organizational knowledge.* New York: Oxford University Press.

Argyris, C. (1996). Actionable knowledge: Design causality in the service of consequential theory. *Journal of Applied Behavioral Science, 32,* 390–406.

Argyris C., & Schön, D. (1996). *Organizational learning II: Theory, method and practice,* Reading, MA: Addison Wesley.

Baker, J. L., Olsen, L. W., & Sorensen, T. I. (2007). Childhood body-mass index and the risk of coronary heart disease in adulthood. *New England Journal of Medicine, 357*(23), 2329–2337.

Bankoff, G., Frerks, G., & Hilhorst, D. (2004). *Mapping vulnerability: Disasters, development and people.* London, UK: Earthscan.

Barnett, E., Anderson, T., Blosnich, J., Menard, J., Halverson, J., & Casper, M. (2007). *Practical Methods—Direct Observations and Windshield Surveys. Heart-Healthy and Stroke- Free: A Social Environment Handbook.* Atlanta: U.S. Department of Health and Human Services, Center for Disease Control and Prevention. Division for Heart Disease and Stroke Prevention.

Bathrellou, E., Yannakoulia, M., Papanikolaou, K., Pehlivanidis, A., Pervanidou, P., Kanaka- Gantenbein, C. et al. (2010). Parental involvement does not augment the effectiveness of an intense behavioral program for the treatment of childhood obesity. *Hormones (Athens), 9*(2), 171–175.

Baum, F., MacDougall, C., Smith, D. (2006). Participatory action research. *Journal of Epidemiology and Community Health, 60*(10): 854–857.

Becker, D., Hogue, A., & Liddle, H. (2002). Methods of engagement in family-based preventive intervention. *Child and Adolescent Social Work Journal, 19*(2), 163–179.

Behar, R. (1997). *The vulnerable observer: Anthropology that breaks your heart.* Boston, MA: Beacon Press.

Bell, J., & Lee, M. (2011). *Why place and race matter: Impacting health through a focus on race and place.* Policy Link. Retrieved on 11/23/13 from http://www.policylink.org/atf/cf/%7B97c6d565-bb43-406d-a6d5eca3bbf35af0%7D/WPRM%20FULL%20REPORT%20%28LORES%29.PDF

Berge, J. M., Mendenhall, T. J., & Doherty, W. J. (2009). Using community-based participatory research (CBPR) To target health disparities in families. *Family Relations, 58*(4), 475–488. DOI: 10.1111/j.1741-3729.2009.00567.x

Berger, P., & Luckmann, T. (1967). *The social construction of reality*. New York: Anchor Books.

Berke, P. R., Kartez, J., & Wenger, D. (1993). Recovery after disaster: Achieving sustainable development, mitigation and equity. *Disasters, 17*(2), 93–109.

Best, A.L. (Ed.). (2007). *Representing youth: Methodological issues in critical youth studies*. New York: New York University Press.

Birch, L. L., & Davison, K. K. (2001). Family environmental factors influencing the developing behavioral controls of food intake and childhood overweight. *Pediatric Clinics of North America, 48*(4), 893–908.

Blaikie, P., Cannon, T., Davis, I., & Wisner, B. (2003). *At risk: Natural hazards, people's vulnerability, and disasters* (2nd ed.). London, UK: Routledge.

Blom-Hoffman, J., Wilcox, K. R., Dunn, L., Leff, S. S., & Power, T. J. (2008). Family Involvement in school-based health promotion: Bringing nutrition information home. *School Psychology Review, 37*(4), 567–577.

Blumenthal, D. (2006). A community coalition board creates a set of values for community based research. *Preventing Chronic Diseases, 3*(1), 1–7.

Boser, S. (2007). Power, ethics, and the IRB dissonance over human participant review of participatory research. *Qualitative Inquiry, 13*(8), 1060–1074.

Bozlak, C.T., & Kelley, M.A. (2010). Youth participation in a community campaign to pass a clean indoor air ordinance. *Health Promotion Practice, 11*(4), 530–540.

Brown, P., Morello-Frosch, R., Brody, J. G., Altman, R. G., Rudel, R. A., Senier, L., Perez, C., & Simpson, R. (2010). Institutional review board challenges related to community-based participatory research on human exposure to environmental toxins: A case study. *Environmental Health, 9*(1), 39.

Brydon-Miller, M. & Greenwood, D. (2006). A re-examination of the relationship between action research and human subjects review process. *Action Research, 4*(1), 117–128.

Burns, D. (2010). *Systemic action research: A strategy for whole system change*. Portland, OR: The Policy Press.

Cammarota, J., & Fine, M. (Ed.) (2008). *Revolutionizing education: Youth participatory action research in motion*. New York, NY: Routledge.

Campbell, K., & Hesketh, K. (2007). Strategies which aim to positively impact on weight, physical activity, diet and sedentary behaviours in children from zero to five years. A systematic review of the literature. *Obesity Reviews, 8*, 327–338.

Cargo, M., & Mercer, S.L. (2008). The value and challenges of participatory research: Strengthening its' practice. *Annual Review of Public Health*, *29*, 325–350.

Caringi, J. & Hardiman, E. (2011). Secondary traumatic stress among child welfare in the United States. *International Journal of Child and Family Welfare*. *14* (2), 50–63.

Caringi, J., & Lawson, H. (under review). Conceptualizing a trauma-informed system for Indian country. Manuscript submitted for publication.

Caringi, J., Lawson, H., & Devlin, M. (2012). Planning for emotional labor and secondary traumatic stress in child welfare organizations. *Journal of Family Strengths*, 12(1), 1–31.

Caringi, J., Strolin-Goltzman, J., Lawson, H., McCarthy, M., Briar-Lawson, K., & Claiborne, N. (2008). Child welfare design teams: An intervention to improve workforce retention and facilitate organizational development. *Research on Social Work Practice*, *18*(6), 565–574.

Castells, M. (1999). *Information technology, globalization, and social development*. Geneva: United Nations Research Institute for Social Development.

Catalano, R.F., Berglund, M. L., Ryan, J.A.M., Lonczak, H. S., & Hawkins J.D. (2004). Positive youth development in the United States: Research findings on evaluations of positive youth development programs. *The Annals of the American Academy of Political and Social Science*, *591*(1), 98–124.

Cattaneo, L.B., & Chapman, A. (2010). The process of empowerment: A model for use in research and practice. *American Psychologist*, *65*(7), 646–659.

Centers for Disease Control and Prevention (CDC). (2013). Vital signs: obesity among low-income, preschool-aged children-United States, 2008-2011. *MMWR. Morbidity and mortality weekly report*, *62*(31), 629.

Centers for Disease Control and Prevention (CDC). (2010). *Best practices user guide: Youth engagement–state and community interventions*. Atlanta: U.S. Department of Health and Human Services, Centers for Disease Control and Prevention, National Center for Chronic Disease Prevention and Health Promotion, Office on Smoking and Health.

Chambers, R. (1997). *Whose reality counts? Putting the last first*. London: Intermediate Technology Publications.

Chambers, R. & Guijt, I. (2011). PRA five years later. In Cornwall, A. (Eds.) *The Participation Reader* (pp. 109–121). London, UK: Zed Books.

Checkoway, B. (2011). What is youth participation? *Children and Youth Services Review*, *33*(2), 340–345.

Checkoway, B., & Guitérrez, L. (Eds.). (2011). *Youth participation and community change*. New York, NY: Routledge.

Checkoway, B., & Guitérrez, L. (Eds.). (2006). Youth participation and community change. *Journal of Community Practice*, *14*(1/2). (Entire issue.)

Checkoway, B., & Richards-Schuster, K. (2006). Youth participation for educational reform in low-income communities of color. In S. Ginwright, P. Noguera, & J. Cammarota (Eds.), *Beyond resistance! Youth activism and community change* (pp. 319–332). New York: Routledge.

Checkoway, B., Allison, T., & Montoya, C. (2005). Youth participation in public policy at the municipal level. *Children and Youth Services Review, 27*(10), 1149–1162.

Chevalier, J.M. and Buckles, D.J. (2013). *Participatory action research: Theory and methods for engaged inquiry.* New York: Routledge.

Chomitz, V. R., McGowan, R., Wendel, M., Sandra A. Williams, S., Cabral, H. Stacey E. King, et al. (2010). Healthy living Cambridge kids: A community-based participatory effort to promote healthy weight and fitness. *Obesity, 18*(S1), S45–S53.

Christen, B. D. (2012). Toward relational empowerment. *American Journal of Community Psychology, 50*(1–2), 114–128.

Claiborne, N., Auerbach, C. Lawrence, C. McGowan, B., Lawson, H., McCarthy, M., et al. (in press). Design teams as an organizational intervention to improve job satisfaction and worker turnover in public child welfare. *Journal of Family Strengths.*

Claiborne, N., & Lawson, H. (2011). A two site case study of consultation to develop supervisory teams in child welfare. *Administration in Social Work, 35*(4), 389–411.

Coleman, P. K., & Hildebrandt Karraker, K. (2000). Parenting self-efficacy among mothers of school-age children: Conceptualization, measurement and correlates. *Family Relations, 49*(1), 13–24.

Collins, C. E., Okely, A. D., Morgan, P. J., Jones, R. A., Burrows, T. L., Cliff, D. P. et al. (2011). Parent diet modification, child activity, or both in obese children: an RCT. *Pediatrics, 127*(4), 619–627. DOI: peds.2010-1518 [pii]

Cornwall, A. (2008). Unpacking "participation:" Models, meanings, and practices. *Community Development Journal, 43*(3), 269–283. DOI: 10.1093/cdj/bsn010

Cornwall, A. (Ed.) (2011). *The participation reader.* London, UK: Zed Books.

Cornwall, A. & Jewkes, R. (1995). What is participatory research? *Social Science Medicine, 41*(12), 1667–1676.

Coupland, H., Maher, L., Enriquez, J., Le, K., Pacheco, V., Pham, A., et al. (2005). Clients or colleagues? Reflections on the process of participatory action research with young injecting drug users. *International Journal of Drug Policy, 16*(3), 191–198.

Cowen, E.L. (2000). Psychological wellness: Some hopes for the future. In D. Cicchetti, J. Rappaport, I. Sandler, & R.P. Weissberg (Eds.), *The promotion of wellness in children and adolescents* (pp. 477–503). Washington DC: Child Welfare League of America.

Creswell, J. W., & Plano-Clark, V. L. (2011). *Designing and conducting mixed methods research* (2nd ed.). Thousand Oaks, CA: Sage Publications, Inc.

Davison, K. K., Jurkowski, J. M., Li, K., Kranz, S., & Lawson, H. A. (2013). A childhood obesity intervention developed by families for families: Results from a pilot study. *International Journal of Behavioral Nutrition and Physical Activity, 10*(3), 1–11.

Davison, K., Lawson, H., & Coatsworth, J. (2012). The Family-centered action model of intervention layout and implementation (FAMILI): The example of childhood obesity. *Health Promotion Practice, 13*(4), 454–461.

Davison, K., Jurkowski, J., & Lawson, H. (2011). Family realities and childhood obesity prevention in low-income families: Testing and refining the family ecological model. *Annals of Behavioral Medicine, 41*, S247–S257.

Davison, K., & Campbell, K. (2005). Opportunities to prevent obesity in children within families: An ecological approach. In D. Crawford & R. Jeffery (Eds.), *Obesity Prevention and Public Health* (pp. 207–230). Oxford: Oxford University Press.

Delgado, M., & Zhou, H. (2008). *Youth-led health promotion in urban communities: A community capacity-enhancement perspective.* Lanham, MD: Rowman & Littlefield.

Dearing, J.W. (2009). Applying diffusion of innovation theory to intervention development. *Research on Social Work Practice, 19*(5): 503–518. DOI:10.1177/1049731509335569.

DiClemente, R.J. Santelli, J.S., & Crosby, R.A. (Eds.) (2009). *Adolescent health: Understanding and preventing risk behaviors.* San Francisco: John Wiley & Sons.

Dietz, W., & Gortmaker, S. (2001). Preventing obesity and children and adolescents. *Annual Review of Public Health, 22*, 337–353.

Dove, M. R., & Huq Khan, M. (1995). Competing constructions of calamity: The April 1991 Bangladesh cyclone. *Population and Environment, 16*(5), pp. 445–471.

Economos, C. D., Hyatt, R. R., Goldberg, J. P., Must, A., Naumova, E. N., Collins, J. J., & Nelson, M. E. (2007). A community intervention reduces BMI z-score in children: Shape Up Somerville first year results. *Obesity (Silver Spring), 15*(5), 1325–1336. DOI: 15/5/1325 [pii]10.1038/oby.2007.155

Economos, C. D., & Irish-Hauser, S. (2007). Community interventions: a brief overview and their application to the obesity epidemic. *J Law Med Ethics, 35*(1), 131–137. DOI: JLME117 [pii] 10.1111/j.1748-720X.2007.00117.x

Education Center for Community Organizing, (N.D.). *Feminist organizing principles.* New York, NY: CUNY Hunter College School of Social Work.

Eisenhardt, K.M. (2002). Building theories from case study research. In A.M. Huberman & M.B. Miles (Eds.), *The qualitative researcher's companion* (pp: 5–36). Thousand Oaks, CA: Sage Publications.

El Ansari, W. (1999). *A study of the characteristics, participant perceptions and predictors of effectiveness in community partnerships in health personnel education: The case of South Africa.* University of Wales College.

Ewald, W. (2001). *I wanna take me a picture.* Boston: Beacon Press.

Fitzgibbon, M. L., Stolley, M. R., Schiffer, L., Van Horn, L., KauferChristoffel, K., & Dyer, A. (2005). Two-year follow-up results for hip-hop to health jr.: A randomized controlled trial for overweight prevention in preschool minority children. *The Journal of Pediatrics, 146*(5), 618–625. DOI: S0022347604011710 [pii]10.1016/j.jpeds.2004.12.019

Fawcett, S. B., Paine-Andrews, A., Francisco, V. T., Schultz, J. A., Richter, K. P., Lewis, R. K.,... & Fisher, J. L. (1996). Empowering community health initiatives through evaluation. In D. Fetterman, S. Kaftarian, & A. Wandersman (Eds.) *Empowerment evaluation: Knowledge and tools for self-assessment and accountability* (pp. 161–187). Thousand Oaks, CA: Sage Publishers.

Fitzgibbon, M. L., Stolley, M. R., Schiffer, L., Van Horn, L., KauferChristoffel, K., & Dyer, A. (2005). Two-year follow-up results for Hip-Hop to Health Jr.: a randomized controlled trial for overweight prevention in preschool minority children. *The Journal of Pediatrics, 146*(5), 618–625.

Flicker, S., Maley, O., Ridgley, A., Biscope, S., Lombardo, C., & Skinner, H. (2008). e-PAR: Using technology and participatory action research to engage youth in health promotion. *Action Research, 6*(3), 285–303.

Fook, J. (2002). *Social work: Critical theory and practice.* London, UK: Sage Publications.

Fordham, M. (1999). The intersection of gender and social class in disaster: Balancing resilience and vulnerability. *International Journal of Mass Emergencies and Disasters, 17*(1), 15–36.

Foster-Fishman, P.G., & Watson, E.R. (2011). The Able change framework: A conceptual and methodological tool for promoting systems change. *American Journal of Community Psychology, 41*, 327–350. DOI: 10.1007/s10464-011-9454-x.

Foster-Fishman, P.G., Law, K.M., Lichty, L.F., & Aoun, C. (2010). Youth reACT for social change: A method for youth participatory action research. *American Journal of Community Psychology, 46*, 67–83.

Foster-Fishman, P. G., & Behrens, T. R. (2007). Systems change reborn: Rethinking our theories, methods, and efforts in human services reform and community-based change. *American Journal of Community Psychology, 39*(3–4), 191–196.

Freire, P. (1974). *Education for critical consciousness.* London: Sheed & Ward Ltd.

Freire, P. (2000). *Pedagogy of the oppressed. 30th Anniversary edition.* New York: Continuum International Publishing Group.

Freire, P. (2003). *Pedagogy of the oppressed.* New York: Continuum International Publishing Group Ltd.

Friedman, V. (2001). Action science: Creating communities of inquiry in communities of practice. In P. Reason & H. Bradbury (Eds.), *Handbook of action research: Participative inquiry and practice* (pp. 159–170). Thousand Oaks, CA: Sage Publishers.

Fullbright-Anderson, K., & Auspos, P. (2006). *Community change: Theories, practice, and evidence.* Washington, DC: Aspen Institute.

Gelmon, S., Malone, R., & Yancey, E. (2007). CCPH/Bioethics Center Educational Conference Call Series on IRBs and Ethical Issues in Research: Call 3 "Community-Based Participatory Research (CBPR) Proposals and the Human Subjects Review Process: Methods for Working with University IRBs."

Ginwright, S., Noguera, P., Cammarota, J. (2006). *Beyond resistance! youth activism and community change.* New York: Routledge.

Glasgow Centre for Population Health. (2011). *Asset based approaches for health improvement: redressing the balance.* (Briefing Paper 9). Retrieved from Glasgow Centre for Population Health website: http://www.gcph.co.uk/assets/0000/2627/GCPH_Briefing_Paper_CS9web.pdf

Glasgow, R. E., & Emmons, K. M. (2007). How can we increase translation of research into practice? Types of evidence needed. *Annual Review of Public Health, 28,* 413–433. DOI: 10.1146/annurev.publhealth.28.021406.144145.

Glisson, C., & Hemmelgarn, A. (1998). The effects of organizational climate and interorganizational coordination the quality and outcomes of children's service systems. *Child Abuse and Neglect, 22*(5), 401–421.

Golan, M. (2006). Parents as agents of change in childhood obesity—from research to practice. *Int J Pediatr Obes, 1*(2), 66–76.

Golan, M., Kaufman, V., & Shahar, D. R. (2006). Childhood obesity treatment: targeting parents exclusively v. parents and children. *Br J Nutr, 95*(5), 1008–1015. DOI: S0007114506001322 [pii]

Granner, M. L., & Sharpe, P. A. (2004). Evaluating community coalition characteristics and functioning: a summary of measurement tools. *Health Education Research, 19*(5), 514–532.

Gray, M., Coates, J., Yellow Bird, M., & Hetherington, J. (2013). *Decolonizing social work.* Burlington, VT: Ashgate Publishing Company.

Greene, S., & Hogan, D. (Eds.) (2005). *Researching children's experience: Approaches and methods.* London: Sage Publications.

Greenwood, D., & Levin, M. (2007). *An introduction to action research.* Thousand Oaks, CA: Sage Publications.

Guha-Sapir, D., & Hoyois, P. (2012). *Measuring the human and economic impact of disasters.* Government Office of Science. Retrieved from http://www.bis.gov.uk/assets/foresight/docs/reducing-risk-management/supporting-evidence/12-1295-measuring-human-economic-impact-disasters.pdf

Gunewardena, N., & Schuller, M. (2008). *Capitalizing on catastrophe: neoliberal strategies in disaster reconstruction.* Lanham, MD: Altamira.

Hackman, J.R. (2012). From causes to conditions in group research. *Journal of Organizational Behavior, 33*(3), 428–444.

Harper, M., & Cole P. (2012). Member-checking: Can benefits be gained similar to group therapy? *The Qualitative Report, 17*(2), 510–517.

Hart, R.A. (1992). *Children's participation: From tokenism to citizenship.* Florence, Italy: UNICEF International Child Development Centre.

Harwell, E. E. (2000). Remote sensibilities: discourses of technology and the making of Indonesia's natural disaster. *Development and Change, 31,* 307–340.

Haslam, P.A., Schafer, J. and Beaudet, P. (2009). *Introduction to international development: approaches, actors and issues.* Don Mills, ON: Oxford University Press.

Heifetz, R.A. (2006). Anchoring leadership in the work of adaptive process. In F. Hesselbein & M. Goldsmith (Eds.), *The leader of the future 2: Visions, strategies, and practices for a new era* (pp. 73–84). San Francisco: Jossey-Bass/John A. Wiley Imprint.

Herr, K., & Anderson, G.L. (2010). *The action research dissertation: A Guide for students and faculty.* 2nd Edition. Thousand Oaks, CA: Sage Publications.

Hingle, M., O'Connor, T., Dave, J., & Baranowski, T. (2010). Parental involvement in interventions to improve child dietary intake: A systematic review. *Preventive Medicine, 51,* 103–111.

Israel, B., Eng, E., Schulz, A., & Parker, E. (2005). *Methods in community-based participatory research for health.* San Francisco, CA: John Wiley & Sons, Inc.

Israel, B.A., Schulz, A.J., Parker, E.A., & Becker, A. (1998). Review of community-based research: Assessing partnership approaches to improve public health. *Annual Review of Public Health, 19,* 173–202.

Israel, B. A., Checkoway, B., Schulz, A., & Zimmerman, M. (1994). Health education and community empowerment: conceptualizing and measuring perceptions of individual, organizational, and community control. *Health Education Quarterly, 21*(2), 149–170.

Johnston-Goodstar, K. (2013). Indigenous youth participatory action research: Reinvisioning social justice for social work with indigenous youths. *Social Work, 58*(4), 314–320.

Joseph, B., Lob, S., McLaughlin, P., Mizrahi, T., Peterson, J., Rosenthal, B. and Sugarman, F. (1991). *A framework for feminist organizing: Values, goals, methods, strategies, and roles.* New York: Education Center for Community Organizing.

Jurkowski, J. (2008). Photovoice as a participatory action research tool for engaging people with intellectual disabilities in research and program development. *Intellectual and Developmental Disabilities, 46*(1), 1–11.

Jurkowski, J. M., Lawson, H. A., Green Mills, L. L., Wilner, P. G.,III & Davison, K. K. (2014). The empowerment of low-income parents engaged in a childhood obesity intervention. *Family & Community Health, 37*(2), 104–118.

Jurkowski, J. M., Green Mills, L. L., Lawson, H. A., Bovenzi, M. C., Quartimon, R., & Davison, K. K. (2013). Engaging low-income parents in childhood obesity prevention from start to finish: a case study. *Journal of Community Health, 38*(1), 1–11. DOI: 10.1007/s10900-012-9573-9

Kaufman, C. (2003). *Ideas for action: Relevant theory for radical change.* Cambridge, MA: South End Press.

Kemmis, S., & McTaggart, R. (2005). Participatory action research: communicative action and the public sphere, in N. K. Denzin & Y. S. Lincoln (Eds.), *The SAGE handbook of qualitative research* (pp. 559–603), 3rd ed. London, UK: Thousand Oaks.

Kemmis, S., & McTaggart, R. (2000). Participatory action research. In N. Denzin & Y. Lincoln (Eds.), *Handbook of qualitative research* (pp. 567–605). Thousand Oaks, CA: Sage Publishers.

Kerner, J.F., & Hall, K.L. (2009). Research dissemination and diffusion: Translation within science and society. *Research on Social Work Practice, 19*(5), 519–530. DOI: 10.1177/1049731509335585.

Kincheloe, J. L., & McLaren, P. (2000). Rethinking critical theory and qualitative research. In N. K. Denzin & Y. S. Lincoln (Eds.), *Handbook of qualitative research* (2nd ed., pp. 279–314). Thousand Oaks, CA: Sage.

Kindon, S., Pain, R., & Kesby, M. (eds.) (2007). *Participatory action research approaches and methods: Connecting people, participation and place.* London, UK: Routledge.

Klein, N. (2007). *The shock doctrine: The rise of disaster capitalism.* New York: Metropolitan Books.

Kretzmann, J., & McKnight, J. (1993). *Building communities from the inside out: A path toward finding and mobilizing a community's assets.* Chicago: ACTA.

Kuhn, T. K. (1996). *The structure of scientific revolutions.* Chicago: University of Chicago Press.

Laverack, G., & Wallerstein, N. (2001). Measuring community empowerment: A fresh look at organizational domains. *Health Promotion International*, 16(2), 179–185.

Lawson, H. (2009). Collaborative practice. In T. Mizrahi & L. Davis, (Eds.), *The encyclopedia of social work* (pp. 341–347). New York: Oxford University Press.

Lawson, H. A. (2011). Collaborative, democratic professionalism aimed at mobilizing citizens to address globalization's challenges and opportunities. In W. Roth & K. Briar-Lawson (Eds.), *Globalization and the helping professions* (pp. 39–67). Albany, NY: SUNY Press.

Lawson, H. A. (2013). Third-generation partnerships for P-16 pipelines and cradle-to-careereducation systems. *Peabody Journal of Education, 88*(5), 637–656. DOI: org/10.1080/0161956X.2013.835187

Lawson, H. (2005). Empowering people, facilitating community development, and contributing to sustainable development: The social work of sport, exercise, and physical education programs. *Sport, Education and Society, 10*(1), 135–160.

Lawson, H., Anderson-Butcher, D., Petersen, N., & Barkdull, C. (2003). Design teams as learning systems for complex systems change: Evaluation data and implications for higher education. *Human Behavior in the Social Environment, 7*(1/2), 159–179.

Lawson, H., & Caringi, J. (2008). *Preparing facilitators for retention-focused design teams*. Albany, NY: Social Work Education Consortium, University at Albany, School of Social Welfare. Available for download at:http://www.ocfs.state.ny.us/ohrd/swec/pubs/DT%20Trainers%20Manual%20FINAL%20formatted.pdf

Lawson, H., Claiborne, N., McCarthy, M., Strolin, J., Briar-Lawson, K., Caringi, J., et al. (2005). *Initiating retention planning in New York State public child welfare agencies: Developing knowledge, lessons learned and emergent priorities*. Albany, NY: The New York State Social Work Education Consortium. http://www.albany.edu/swec/resources_publications/pdfs/Five%20Year%20Compendium%20of%20SWEC%20Work%20(2005).pdf

Lawson, H. A., McCarthy, M., Briar-Lawson, K., Miraglia, P., Strolin, J., & Caringi, J. (2006). A complex partnership to optimize and stabilize the public child welfare workforce. *Professional Development: The International Journal of Continuing Social Work Education, 9*(2–3), 122–139.

Lawson, H., Petersen, N., & Briar-Lawson, K. (2001). From conventional training to empowering design teams for collaboration and systems change. In A. Sallee, H. Lawson, & K. Briar-Lawson (Eds.), *Innovative practices with vulnerable children and families* (pp. 361–392). Dubuque, IA: Eddie Bowers Publishers, Inc.

Leadbeater, B., Banister, E., Benoit, C., Jansson, M., Marshall, A., & Riecken, T. (Ed.) (2006). *Ethical issues in community-based research with children and youth*. Toronto: University of Toronto Press.

Leamer, L. (2001). *The Kennedy men: 1901:1963*. New York: Harper Collins.

Leff, S.S., Thomas, D.E., Vaughn, N.A., Thomas, N.A., Paquette MacEvoy, J., Freedman, M.A., et al. (2010). Using community-based participatory research to develop the PARTNERS youth violence prevention program. *Progress in Community Health Partnerships: Research, Education, and Action, 4*(3), 207–216.

Levy, S. R., Baldyga, W., & Jurkowski, J. M. (2003). Developing community health promotion interventions: selecting partners and fostering collaboration. *Health Promotion Practice, 4*(3), 314–322.

Lewin, K. (1951). *Field theory in social science; Selected theoretical papers.* D. Cartwright (Ed.). New York: Harper & Row.

Lindsay, A. C., Sussner, K. M., Greaney, M. L., & Peterson, K. E. (2009). Influence of social context on eating, physical activity, and sedentary behaviors of Latina mothers and their preschool-age children. *Health Education & Behavior, 36*(1), 81–96.

Lindsay, A. C., Sussner, K. M., Kim, J., & Gortmaker, S. (2006). The role of parents in preventing childhood obesity. *Future of Children, 16*(1), 169–186.

Lipsky, M. (1980). *Street-level bureaucracy: Dilemmas of the individual in public services*. New York: Russell Sage Foundation.

Luig, U. (Ed.). (2012). *Negotiating disasters: Politics, representation, meanings.* Frankfurt am Main: Peter Lang.

Lykes, M. B. (2013). Participatory and action research as a transformative praxis: Responding to humanitarian crises from the margins. *American Psychologist, 68*(8), 774–783.

Manning, S. S. (1997). The social worker as moral citizen: Ethics in action. *Social Work, 42*(3), 223–230.

Marks, M. B. (2012). Time banking service exchange systems: A review of research and policy and practice implications in support of youth in transition. *Children and Youth Services Review, 24*, 1230–1236.

Maschi, T., & Youdin, R. (2012). *Social worker as researcher: Integrating with advocacy.* New York: Pearson Education Publishing.

Masuda, J., Creighton, G., Nixon, S., & Frankish, J. (2011). Building capacity for community-based participatory research for health disparities in Canada: The case of "partnerships in community health research." *Health Promotion Practice, 12*(2), 280–292.

May, L. A., Pan, L., Sherry, B., Blanck, H. M., Galuska, D., Dalenius, K., Polhamus, B., Kettel-Khan, L., Grummer-Strawn, L. M. (2013). *Vital signs: Obesity among low-income, preschool-aged children—United States,*

2008-2011. Atlanta: National Center for Chronic Disease Prevention and Health Promotion, CDC.

McCain, G., & Segal, E. (1982). *The game of science*. Independence, KY: Brooks-Cole.

McCallum, Z., Wake, M., Gerner, B., Baur, L. A., Gibbons, K., Gold, L., et al. (2007). Outcome data from the LEAP (live, eat and play) trial: A randomized controlled trial of a primary care intervention for childhood overweight/mild obesity. *International Journal of Obesity, 31*(4), 630–636. DOI: 0803509 [pii]10.1038/sj.ijo.0803509

McTaggart, Robin (2002). *Action research scholar: The role of the scholar in action research*. In M.P. Wolfe & C. Pryor (Eds.). *The mission of the scholar: Research & practice-a tribute to Nelson Haggerson* (pp. 1–16). Counterpoints, 183. New York: Peter Lang Publishing.

Mills, G.E. (2013). *Action research: A guide for the teacher researcher*. Upper Saddle River, NJ: Pearson Education.

Minkler, M. (Ed.). (2012). *Community organizing and community building for health and welfare*. New Brunswick, NJ: Rutgers University Press.

Minkler, M. (2000). Using participatory action research to build healthy communities. *Public Health Reports, 115*(2–3), 191–197.

Minkler, M., & Wallerstein, N. (2003). Introduction to community based participatory research. In M. Minkler & N. Wallerstein (Eds.), *Community based participatory research for health* (pp. 3–26). San Francisco, CA: Jossey-Bass.

Minkler, M., & Cox, K. (1980). Creating critical consciousness in health: applications of Freire's philosophy and methods to the health care setting. *International Journal of Health Services, 10*(2), 311–322.

Morabia, A., & Costanza, M. C. (2010). Engaging parents and children in designing child health research. *Prev Med, 51*(2), 101–102. DOI: S0091-7435(10)00243-4 [pii] 10.1016/j.ypmed.2010.06.016

Morgan, A., & Ziglio, E. (2007). Revitalizing the evidence base for public health: An assets model. *Health Promotion & Education, 14*(Supplement 2), 17–22.

Morin, S. F., Maiorana, A., Koester, K. A., Sheon, N. M., & Richards, T. A. (2003). Community consultation in HIV prevention research: A study of community advisory boards at 6 research sites. *Journal of Acquired Immune Deficiency Syndromes, 33*(4), 513–520.

N.A. (2011). *Early Childhood Obesity Prevention Policies*. Washington, DC: Institute of Medicine.

Nader, P. R., O'Brien, M., Houts, R., Bradley, R., Belsky, J., Crosnoe, R., et al. (2006). Identifying risk for obesity in early childhood. *Pediatrics, 118*(3), 594–601.

National Institute of Medicine. (2011). *Early childhood obesity prevention policies.* Washington, DC: Author.

Norris, F. H., Galea, S., Friedman, M., & Watson, P. (Eds.). (2006). *Methods for disaster mental health research.* New York, NY: Guilford Press.

Nygreen, K. (2009–2010). Critical dilemmas in PAR: Toward a new theory of engaged research for social change. *Social Justice, 36*(4), 14–35.

Oliver-Smith, A. & Hoffman, S.M. (Eds.) (1999). *The angry earth: Disaster in anthropological perspective.* New York: Routledge.

Ozer, E.J., & Wright, D. (2012). Beyond school spirit: The effects of youth-led participatory action research in two urban high schools. *Journal of Research on Adolescence, 22*(2), 267–283.

Patton, M.Q. (2002). *Qualitative research and evaluation methods.* (3rd Ed.). Thousand Oaks, CA: Sage Publications.

Philliber, S. (1998). The virtue of specificity in theory of change evaluation: Practitioner reflections. In K. Fullbright-Anderson, A. Kubisch, & J. Connell (Eds.), *New approaches to evaluating community initiatives, Volume 2: Theory, measurement, and analysis* (pp. 87–99). Queenstown, MD: The Aspen Institute.

Preskill, H., & Beer, T. (2012). *Evaluating social innovation.* Boston: FSG Center for Evaluation Innovation. Downloaded December 3, 2012 from http://www. fsg.org/Portals/0/Uploads/Documents/PDF/Evaluating_Social_Innovatio n.pdf

Preskill, H., & Jones, N. (2009). *A practical guide for engaging stakeholders in developing evaluation questions.* Princeton, NJ: Robert Wood Johnson Foundation.

Prilleltensky, I., & Fox, D.R. (2007). Psychopolitical literacy for wellness and justice. *Journal of Community Psychology, 35*(6), 793–805.

Prinz, R. J., Smith, E. P., Dumas, J. E., Laughlin, J. E., White, D. W., & Barrón, R. (2001). Recruitment and retention of participants in prevention trials involving family-based interventions. *American Journal of Preventive Medicine, 20*(1), 31–37.

Pyles, L. (Under review). Critical reflections on participation in participatory action research in post-earthquake rural Haiti. *International Social Work.*

Pyles, L. (2013). *Progressive community organizing: reflective practice in a globalizing world,* 2nd ed. New York: Routledge.

Pyles, L. (2011). Neoliberalism, INGO practices and sustainable disaster recovery: A post-Katrina case study. *Community Development Journal, 46*(2), 168–180.

Pyles, L. and Harding, S. (2012). Discourses of post-Katrina reconstruction: A frame analysis. *Community Development Journal, 47*(3), 335–352.

Pyles, L., Rodrigue, C., & Andre, J. (2011, November). *Resisting supply-driven approaches to disaster recovery and development through participatory action research in rural Haiti*. Kingston, Jamaica: Haitian Studies Association.

Quane, J.M., & Wilson, W.J. (2012). Critical commentary: Making the connection between the socialization and the social inclusion of the inner-city poor. *Urban Studies, 49*(14), 2977–2987.

Quiroz, P.A., Milam-Brooks, K., Adams-Romena, D. (2014). School as solution to the problem of urban place: Student migration, perceptions of safety, and children's concept of community. *Childhood, 21*(2), 207–225

Raby, R. (2007). Across a great gulf? Conducting research with adolescents. In Best, A. (Ed.), *Representing youth: Methodological issues in critical youth studies* (pp. 39–59). New York: New York University Press.

Reason, P., & Bradbury, H. (2001). *Handbook of action research: Participative inquiry and practice*. London: Sage Publications.

Reason, P., & Bradbury, H. (2001). Introduction: Inquiry and participation in search of a world worthy of human aspiration. In P. Reason & H. Bradbury (Eds.), *Handbook of action research: Participative inquiry and practice* (pp. 1–14). London, UK: Sage Publications.

Reason, P. (2011). Cooperative inquiry. In Cornwall, A. (Ed.), *The participation reader* (pp. 99–108). London, UK: Zed Books.

Reisch, M. and Andrews, J. (2002). *The road not taken: A history of radical social work in the United States*. New York: Brunner-Routledge.

Regher, C. (2000). Action research: Underlining or undermining the Cause? *Social Work and Social Sciences Review, 8*(3), 194–206.

Rodwell, M. (1998). *Social work constructivist research*. New York, NY: Garland Publishing Inc.

Rotegard, A.K., Moore, S.M., Fagermoen, M.S., & Ruland, C.M. (2010). Health assets: A concept analysis. *International Journal of Nursing Studies, 47*(4), 513–525.

Rothman, J., & Thomas E. J. (Eds.). (2009). *Intervention research: Design and development for human services*. New York: Routledge.

Roulier, M. (2000). Reconnecting communities and their schools through authentic dialogue. *National Civic Review, 89*(1), 53–65.

Sakamoto, I., & Pitner, R.O. (2005). Use of critical consciousness in anti-oppressive social work practice: Disentangling power dynamics at personal and structural levels. *British Journal of Social Work, 35*(4), 435–452.

Sallis, J. F., & Glanz, K. (2006). The role of built environments in physical activity, eating, and obesity in childhood. *The Future of Children, 16*(1), 89–108.

Sampson, R.J. (2012). *Great American city: Chicago and the enduring neighborhood effect*. Chicago: University of Chicago Press.

Sandoval, J.A., Lucero, J., Oetzel, J., Avila, M., Belone, L., Mau, M., et al. (2011). Process and outcome constructs for evaluating community-based participatory research projects: A matrix of existing measures. *Health Education Research*, *27*(4), 680–690., DOI: 10.1093/her/cyr087.

Schafft, K., & Greenwood, D. (2003). The promises and dilemmas of participation: Action research, search conference methodology, and community development. *Journal of the Community Development Society*, *34*(1), 18–35.

Schneider, J. (2014). *Participatory action research from A to Z: A comprehensive guide*. Bonita Springs, FL: Principal Investigators Association.

Schön, D. (1983). *The reflective practitioner: How professionals think in action*. New York: Basic Books.

Schuller, M. (2007). Invasion or infusion? Understanding the role of NGOs in contemporary Haiti. *The Journal of Haitian Studies*, *13*(2), pp. 96–119.

Schuller, M. & Morales, P. (Eds.) (2012). *Tectonic shifts: Haiti since the earthquake*. Sterling, VI: Kumarian Press.

Schulz, A. J., Israel, B. A., & Lantz, P. (2003). Instrument for evaluating dimensions of group dynamics within community-based participatory research partnerships. *Evaluation and Program Planning*, *26*(3), 249–262.

Searle, J. (1995). *The construction of social reality*. New York: The Free Press.

Seibert, K., & Daudelin, M. (1999). *The role of reflection in managerial learning: Theory, research, and practice*. Westport, CT: Quorum.

Seidman, S. (2012). An emerging action science of social settings. *American Journal of Community Psychology*, *50*, 1–16. DOI: 10.1007/s10464-011-9469-3

Shiva, V. (2000). Ecological balance in an era of globalization. In F.J. Lechner & I. Boli, J. (Eds.) *The globalization reader* (pp. 422–429), 2nd ed. Malden, MA: Blackwell Publishing.

Shore, N., Drew, E., Brazauskas, R., & Seifer, S. (2011). Relationships betweencommunity-based processes for research ethics review and institution-based IRBs: A national study. *Journal of Empirical Research on Human Research Ethics*, *101*, 13–21.

Sluyter, G. (1998). *Improving organizational performance: A practical guidebook for the human services field*. Sage Human Services Guide 74. Thousand Oaks, CA: Sage Publications.

Smith, L., & Romero, L. (2010). Psychological interventions in the context of poverty: Participatory action research as practice. *American Journal of Orthopsychiatry*, *80*(1), 12–25.

Spoth R., R. C., Hockaday C., Shin C. (1996). Barriers to participation in family skills preventive interventions and their evaluations: A replication and extension. *Family Relations*, *45*(3), 247–254.

St. John, E.P. (2013). Research, actionable knowledge, and social change: Reclaiming responsibility through research partnerships. Sterling, VA: Stylus.

Stevenson, M. (n.d.) 'Voices for Change': Participatory action research in partnership with young adult with down syndrome in New South Wales. ASSID Conference Paper. Retrieved from: www.asid.asn.au/.../ASSID%20 Conference%20paper-Voices%20for%20

Stokols, D. (2000). Social ecology and behavioral medicine: Implications for training, practice, and policy. Behavioral Medicine, 26(3), 129–138.

Strolin-Goltzman, J., Lawrence, C., Auerbach, C., Caringi, J., Claiborne, N., Lawson, H., & Shim, M. (2009). Design teams: A promising organizational intervention for improving turnover rates in the child welfare workforce. Child Welfare, 88(5), 149–168.

Stuttaford, M., & Coe, C. (2007). The "learning" component of participatory learning and action in health research: Reflections from a local sure start evaluation. Qualitative Health Research, 17(10), 1351–1360.

Strack, R.W., Magill, C., & McDonagh, K. (2004). Engaging youth through photovoice. Health Promotion Practice, 5(1), 49–58.

Stringer, E. (2014). Action research. 4th edition. Thousand Oaks, CA: Sage Publishers.

Suglia, S. F., Duarte, C. S., Chambers, E. C., & Boynton-Jarrett, R. (2012). Cumulative social risk and obesity in early childhood. Pediatrics. Pediatrics, 129(5), e1173-e1179.

Sunderland, N., Catalano, R., Kendall, E., McAuliffe, D., & Chenowether, L. (2010). Exploring the concept of moral distress with community-based researchers: An Australian study. Journal of Social Service Research, 37(1), 73–85.

Svistova, J., Pyles, L., & André, J. (in press). The meaning and possibilities of participation in research in Haiti: A case of counter-hegemonic resistance. Social Development Issues Journal.

Symes, J. and Jasser, S. (2011). Growing from the grassroots: building participatory planning, monitoring and evaluation methods in PARC. In Cornwall, A. (Ed.) The participation reader (pp. 125–130). London, UK: Zed Books.

Tigges, L. M., Browne, I., & Green, G. P. (1998). Social isolation of the urban poor. The Sociological Quarterly, 39(1), 53–77.

Trickett, E. (2011). Community-based participatory research as worldview or instrumental strategy: Is it lost in translation(al) research? American Journal of Public Health, 101(8), 1353–1355.

Trickett, E., & Espino, S. (2004). Collaboration and social inquiry: Multiple meanings of a construct and its role in creating useful and valid knowledge. American Journal of Community Psychology, 34(1/2), 1–69.

Tuckman, B. W., & Jensen, M. A. (1977). Stages of small-group development revisited. *Group & Organization Management, 2*(4), 419–427.

U.S. Census Bureau. (2010). *New York Quick Facts from the US Census Bureau* (Vol. 2010).

U.S. Department of Health and Human Services. (2006). *The health consequences of involuntary exposure to tobacco smoke: A report of the Surgeon General— Executive summary.* Rockville, MD: U.S. Department of Health and Human Services, Centers for Disease Control and Prevention, Coordinating Center for Health Promotion, National Center for Chronic Disease Prevention and Health Promotion, Office on Smoking and Health.

Vaughn, K., & Waldrop, J. (2007). Childhood obesity. Part II. Parent education key to beating early childhood obesity. *The Nurse practitioner, 32*(3), 36–41; quiz 41-33. DOI: 10.1097/01.NPR.0000263086.16643.03 00006205-200703000-00014 [pii]

Wadsworth, Y. (2010). *Building in research and evaluation: Human inquiry for living systems.* Walnut Creek, CA: Left Coast Press, Inc.

Wang, C. C. (2003). Using photovoice as a participatory assessment and issue selection tool: A case study with the homeless in Ann Arbor. In M. Minkler & N. Wallerstein (Eds.), *Community-based participatory research for health* (pp. 180–196). San Francisco: Jossey-Bass.

Wang, C. C. (1999). Photovoice: A participatory action research strategy applied to women's health. *Journal of Women's Health, 8*(2), 185–192.

Wang, C., & Burris, M. A. (1997). Photovoice: concept, methodology, and use for participatory needs assessment. *Health Educ Behav, 24*(3), 369–387.

Waterman, H. (1998). Embracing ambiguities and valuing ourselves: Issues of validity in action research. *Journal of Advanced Nursing, 28*(1), 101–105.

Watts, R., Diemer, M., & Voigt, A. (2011). Critical consciousness and sociopolitical development: Current status & future directions. In C. Flanagan, & B. Christens (Eds.), *Youth civic development: Work at the cutting edge: New directions for child and adolescent development* (134th ed., pp. 43–58). Hoboken, NJ: Wiley.

Watts, R., & Flanagan, C. (2007). Pushing the envelope on youth civic engagement: A developmental and liberation psychology perspective. *Journal of Community Psychology, 35*(6), 779–792.

Weick, K. (1984). Small wins: Redefining the scale of social problems. *American Psychologist, 39*(1), 40–49.

Whitaker, R., & Orzol, S. (2006). Obesity among US urban preschool children. *Archives of Pediatrics and Adolescent Medicine, 160,* 578–584.

Whitaker, R. C., Wright, J. A., Pepe, M. S., Seidel, K. D., & Dietz, W. H. (1997). Predicting obesity in young adulthood from childhood and parental obesity. *New England Journal of Medicine, 337*(13), 869–873.

W.K. Kellogg Foundation. (2004). *Logic model development guide*. Retrieved from: http://www.wkkf.org/resource-directory/resource/2006/02/wk-kellogg-foundation-logic-model-development-guide

Wolch, J., Jerrett, M., Reynolds, K., McConnell, R., Chang, R., Dahmann, N., et al. (2011). Childhood obesity and proximity to urban parks and recreational resources: A longitudinal cohort study. *Health & Place, 17*(1), 207–214.

World Health Organization. (2014). *The Ottawa charter for health promotion*. First International Conference on Health Promotion. Retrieved from: http://www.who.int/healthpromotion/conferences/previous/ottawa/en/

World Health Organization. (2014). *Tobacco free initiative*. Retrieved from: http://www.who.int/tobacco/en/

Zimmerman, M. A., & Rappaport, J. (1988). Citizen participation, perceived control, and psychological empowerment. *American Journal of Community Psychology, 16*(5), 725–750.

Index

Printed in the USA
CPSIA information can be obtained
at www.ICGtesting.com
LVHW010848080824
787594LV00001B/54